Listen to the Silence
A Retreat with Père Jacques

Listen to the Silence
A Retreat with Père Jacques

Translated and Edited by
Francis J. Murphy

ICS Publications
Institute of Carmelite Studies
Washington, D.C.
2005

This work is taken from an original typescript.

Translation authorized by Discalced Carmelites, Province of Paris.

www.icspublications.org

Cover design by Rosemary Moak, O.C.D.S.
Typesetting by Stephen Tiano Page Design & Production
Typeset and produced in the U.S.A.

Library of Congress Cataloging-in-Publication Data

Jacques, père. 1900-1945.
Listen to the silence : a retreat with Père Jacques / translated and edited by Francis J. Murphy.
p. cm.
Includes bibliographical references.
ISBN 0-935216-34-0 (alk. paper)
1. Discalced Carmelite Nuns—Spiritual life. 2. Spiritual life—Catholic Church. I. Murphy, Francis J. II. Title.
BX4322.J22 2004
248.8'943—dc22
2004006397

Contents

Pontoise Monastery Entrance

Preface

This work has been facilitated by the gentle guidance and generous assistance of many colleagues in both France and United States. To each of them I express my fullest appreciation. In addition, the special contributions of certain individuals deserve personal acknowledgment.

I want to thank Catherine Marais, secretary of the original Comité Père Jacques, for first introducing me to the text of the Pontoise retreat. As the project of translating and editing the retreat advanced, I wish to acknowledge with gratitude the assistance of Elisabeth Frébourg, who shared with me her expertise regarding the preaching of Père Jacques; Sister Margaret McCarthy, S.C.H., whose mastery of French brought clarity to several complex passages of the text; and Sister Joanne Kmiec, whose computer skills proved invaluable in locating the sources of many quotations used by Père Jacques.

I am doubly grateful to Sister Marie Jeanne, Prioress of the Carmel of Pontoise, who warmly welcomed me there in August 2000 and who subsequently supplied me with both invaluable information and photographs. My fullest thanks are with the members of the Institute for Carmelite Studies, especially Friars Steven Payne and John Sullivan, who have encouraged and assisted me from the inception to the completion of this project. I can not adequately acknowledge the role of Monsignor Laurence McGrath, who made completely available to me not only the rich resources of the Saint John's Seminary Library (Brighton, MA) but also his own inexhaustible knowledge of Church history.

Finally, I want to thank Karen Potterton, secretary of the History Department at Boston College, who cheerfully and expertly prepared the manuscript of this work through its many drafts to its final form.

Unless otherwise indicated, all translations from French are mine. Scripture texts are drawn from the New American Bible. The inspiring content of this Retreat at Pontoise is part of the enduring legacy of Père Jacques. If his deep spirituality becomes better known through this study, then the work will certainly have achieved its goal, despite any shortcomings on my part.

Francis J. Murphy
July, 2002

Introduction

Père Jacques is remembered today primarily for his heroic role in the French Resistance to Nazism. His efforts to rescue Jewish students from deportation and death at the hands of the Nazis have been heralded in the award-winning film, "Au revoir, les enfants." His willingness to risk and eventually to give up his life in order to help the Jewish victims of Nazi persecution has been recognized by the government of Israel, which awarded him posthumously the title, "Righteous among the Nations."

During his life, prior to his arrest and imprisonment by the Nazis, Père Jacques was regarded by his contemporaries as a remarkably respected educator and an exceptionally dedicated Carmelite priest. He was especially esteemed as a preacher. As a young priest, he had made a personal pledge never to refuse an invitation to preach. He had, in this capacity, a special rapport with the communities of Carmelite nuns in France.

The Carmel of Pontoise, approximately twenty miles northwest of Paris, dates back to 1605 and is the oldest, continuously operating Carmelite community in France. Père Jacques first visited the Carmel of Pontoise in 1923, when he was a student at the Seminary of Rouen. Lucien Bunel, the future Père Jacques, had just completed his military service. While in the service, he had read the autobiography of Sister Marie-Angélique, a celebrated Carmelite nun, who had died in the convent at Pontoise in 1919. His visit to the Carmel of Pontoise was young Lucien

Bunel's first serious experience of Carmelite life. It would not be an exaggeration to say that the seeds of his Carmelite calling were sown at Pontoise.

On January 2, 1944, Père Jacques returned to Pontoise to present a conference on Sister Marie-Angélique. Two weeks later, on January 15, Père Jacques was arrested along with the three Jewish students, whom he had sheltered at the Petit-Collège in Avon. Neither Père Jacques nor any of the captured Jewish students ever returned from the Nazi camps. That conference at Pontoise was the last ever given by Père Jacques. In this light, Pontoise was the site of both the dawn and the twilight of Père Jacques's life as a Carmelite.

Père Jacques had maintained close ties with the Carmel of Pontoise for twenty years and his presence there for the community retreat in September 1943 proved to be the culmination of that relationship. The text of the conferences of that retreat has been preserved in a curiously providential way. We know that, except on very formal occasions, Père Jacques preferred to preach from an outline or hand-written notes. However, when the cause of the beatification of Père Jacques was launched in 1990, an appeal was made to all the Carmelite communities of France to search for any letters or documents relating to Père Jacques. Among the materials provided by the Carmel of Pontoise was the full type-written transcription of the retreat given by Père Jacques to the Carmelite sisters there in September 1943.

It was the custom of that era, before the invention of tape recorders, for one of the sisters in the community to record the retreat conferences in shorthand and subsequently to type up her notes. Then copies of the text of each conference would be given to all the sisters for their further reflection and meditation. The resulting transcription is, on the whole, remarkably complete. Needless to say, the insertion of punctuation, that could alter the sense of a sentence, was done by the stenographer. Likewise, the title of each conference was supplied by the typist. Occasionally, when there is some ambiguity or apparent addition to the text, I have so indicated in the accompanying notes.

The format of the retreat conforms to the standard of the time. There were two conferences each day, one after morning Mass and the other prior to evening prayer. The content of the retreat conferences is simultaneously classically Carmelite and pastorally contemporary. In addition to his frequent references to the great Carmelite spiritual writers, Père Jacques stresses such characteristically Carmelite themes as prayer, poverty, obedience and, above all, silence. His use of sacred Scripture, his emphasis on the Eucharist and his advocacy of social justice all reflect the dynamic renewal of French Catholicism in the wake of World War I.

Almost sixty years have passed since Père Jacques directed the retreat conferences at the Carmel of Pontoise in September 1943. The rich spiritual content of those conferences and their practical applicability are as timely today as they were then. God still speaks in the silence.

Buildings seen from Monastery Garden

Conference 1
Solitude, the Essence of Carmel
Monday, September 6, 1943

Before considering what will be presented in this retreat, dear Sisters, let us together place ourselves in God's presence.[1] No good will be accomplished in our souls, unless God[2] himself is at work within us. A human person will be speaking to you during this retreat. That person is a priest, who is striving to live out his priesthood authentically and faithfully. He is a priest who has put himself totally at the disposal of God.

Since God is invisible he needs intermediaries who lend him their lips, their bodies, their hearts and their minds. The priest is such a person. By a kind of "surrender of his own personality," the priest puts his whole being at the disposal of God. The priest should then say only what God wishes to be said. Therefore, do not focus on the human person who will be speaking to you. Rather, listen to the voice of God and you will discover, at one moment or another, something amazing. The message of the retreat will prove to be so applicable to your needs, your present situation, and your personal concerns, that you will have the impression that the retreat master is speaking to you and you alone, without being aware of it.

Let us now place ourselves in God's presence, so that he can speak personally to each one of you. Let us all do our duty. I want to fulfill my duty to let God speak to you through the words he puts on my lips and the ideas he places in my mind, without mincing his message. Likewise, it is your duty to welcome the message of our retreat as coming not from a man, but from God. Together, let us be totally honest and straightforward in our shared search for truth. At the end of our retreat, we want to be able to repeat the beautiful words of Cardinal Newman, a convert from Protestantism, who said: "I have not sinned against light."[3]

Let us be aware that God is here present among us. Let us gaze upon him in and around us. Let us likewise place ourselves in the presence of the Virgin Mary, our model of contemplation, who listened faithfully to God throughout her life. Let us ask her to teach us how to listen to God, to grasp his words, and to live them out. Let us pray to the saints of our own religious family, the Carmelites. Let us place ourselves in their presence, so that our retreat may bring us all its anticipated fruits, and we may go forth spiritually renewed. Indeed, spiritual renewal is a life-long requirement.

We are entering into retreat. I say "we" are entering into retreat, because I am going to make my retreat together with you. The word retreat means literally to "retire" or to "draw back." This concept of retreat should be dear to us. Otherwise we would not be here in a cloistered convent. Each one of you remembers, don't you, how you first experienced this need for retreat, which is at the root of your vocation and your desire to enter the silence of the cloister? There was an inner stirring, a deep spiritual need that little by little impelled every entrant to Carmel. The one, authentic Carmel consists of a quiet, uninterrupted conversation with God. That is the true Carmel that our Carmelite forebears sought. We can neither find nor embrace God, just as we cannot sit at his feet in order to gaze lovingly upon him, if we are immersed in noise and activity. We cannot hear the voice of God, who speaks without words, except in silence.

Consider the example of our spiritual father, Elijah.[4] Note the eagerness with which he returned from his apostolic activities to his beloved cave at Carmel. It was solitude that he sought in order to replenish his spirit through silent intimacy with God. Consider how all the luminaries of our religious family teach us the same lesson. Saint John of the Cross[5] entered religious life in response to his powerful attraction toward retreat and away from the world. However, his first experience of solitude proved to be insufficient. The world still readily intruded into his life through visitors and conversation. That level of retreat did not satisfy his deepest spiritual need. In the recesses of his heart, there arose a longing for another type of retreat, that of la Chartreuse.[6] This need to withdraw from the world and to undertake total retreat penetrated the depths of his being. When Saint Teresa urged him to remain a Carmelite and to establish a community consistent with his inclination, he replied: "I would gladly do so, but life passes quickly."[7] Such was his sense of urgency to find a place of retreat that would fulfill all the burning desire of his lively soul in its quest to find God.

Likewise, consider Saint Thérèse of Lisieux.[8] The need for silence and solitude burned within her. However, the monastery that she entered was not the object of her dreams. She longed for the day when the spirit, the Rule, and the silence of Carmel would be fully restored. There she could live the life of Carmel in all its depth. This is the lesson that she teaches to her novices. We, too, submitted to that deep spiritual impulse on the day God touched our life, perhaps after receiving Communion or during an hour of deep prayer. At that moment we felt, understood, and lived the truth that God is not a word, but rather a living being, who envelops us. He made us aware in the depths of our souls that this first living personal contact was with the very being of God. We wanted to prolong and to intensify this presence of God. We acted upon this desire and thus we entered the monastery. Here, we speak again and again of retreat. We speak of monthly and annual retreat, individual and community retreat–always retreat. Let us strip ourselves of our illusions and love the truth with steadfast sincerity. When we entered the monastery, we left everything behind us, even our families and our possessions. You remember the example of Sister Marie Angélique: when she left her piano behind her, she felt her fingers stiffen.[9]

We have left behind all our possessions. However, we have entered religious life with our personalities and our identities, our bodies and our hearts, our minds and our memories intact. None of these have been left behind. We cannot root out our memories nor stifle our intellectual curiosity. We cannot strip our bodies of their instincts nor our selves of their identity.

The author of the *Imitation of Christ*[10] tells us that there is no point in going off in solitude on retreat, if we do not leave the self behind. It is an illusion to think that we will be better elsewhere, as if somehow we leave our problems behind, when we change our location. When one leaves a particular place, the totality of that person leaves, including a bit of the world. There remain within us the sounds, the impressions, and the passions of the world, as well as its capacity for evil, envy and egotism. Therefore, our retreat must be directed toward not one particular day, such as our profession, but rather toward our entire life.

Do you remember the instructions of our holy father Saint John of the Cross, when he depicted Carmel using the symbol of a mountain? At the summit, he put the goal of our life; he mapped out the withdrawal from the world that we must undertake to arrive at this point of all-embracing union with God. In the middle was a steep path; on each side, he sketched the easier routes, which were makeshift and incomplete. Then, between them, with a quick stroke, he drew what must be the way of our retreat; a direct, exacting road on which one hears the refrain "Nothing, nothing, absolutely nothing but God alone."[11] Not this little personal matter, not this slight comfort we cling to, not this tiny curiosity that seems so trivial, but "nothing, absolutely nothing"—John of the Cross is speaking. You see, this retreat we are making must have direction. When Saint Bernard arrived at the monastery, he too asked himself frequently: "Bernard, what did you come to the monastery to do?"[12]

Each morning, when we come down to choir to pray, this must be the question we ask. We came to the monastery to escape the noise and distractions of the world in order to find God and not ourselves. The prioress of the Carmel of Toulouse, I believe, was asked: "What purpose do these Carmels serve?" She replied: "They serve to reveal God!" This reply is sublime, it is true, and there is no way to deny it.

Carmel is a community of human beings who reveal God to other human beings. There should be a Carmel in every city, and then there would be no need of works. One would see God through these human beings who live for him and him alone.

A person does not withdraw to Carmel because of weariness, or to know tranquillity, or to live a mediocre life, or to flee the cares of keeping a home and family, or to have a more comfortable existence. One comes here because she is athirst for God, because she desires to find God and to reveal God to the whole world.

In reading the history of the Church or the history of our own order, like all the other orders, except for the Carthusians, we find periods of decline and need of reform in the wake of intervals of laxity and even scandal. Even among priests and religious, we find cases of spiritual death. We learn that a particular priest grew spiritually cold and left the priesthood, only to embark upon a life of degradation. You need to be aware of such cases and, in turn, to pray for priests. As you can see, it is not enough to experience a period of surpassing spiritual fervor. Gradually, one can abandon retreat instead of intensifying it. Gradually, one can return to the world left behind by readopting its norms instead of embracing God's standards ever more fully.

For all these reasons, the Church calls for all religious communities to redouble their retreat at certain times. That is precisely what we are going to do together this week. We are going to do so by entering into greater intimacy with God, whom Saint Teresa of Avila urges us to grasp more fully. We are going to spend this week in close union with Christ by fixing our gaze upon him, as John the Apostle and Mary did at the foot of the cross. We are going to focus on the beauty and immensity of Christ's extraordinary being. We are going to search out the secrets of his double nature and divine personality. We will listen to his advice. We will observe him praying, loving and saving souls. At the side of his mother, the Virgin Mary, we will share his confidences.

At the close of our retreat, our souls should be burning with love for Christ. It was for Christ that we entered here. It is for Christ that we live in such a way that each consecrated religious can be called "Bride of the Word." Therefore, let us plunge fully into our retreat and make it wholeheartedly, not lackadaisically. Let us seek, not emotional satisfaction, but rather a passionate love of truth and light. Let us make that light shine within us, within our monastery, and within our religious family so that we may seek Christ in loving silence. Then let us grasp his hand and hold it firmly until that blessed moment when we can see, face to face and eye to eye, him whom we did our best to find here on earth. Amen.

Conference 2
Christ, the Object of Our Prayer
Monday Evening

If we have allowed our soul to become somewhat distracted during the course of the day, let us now peacefully place ourselves once again in the presence of God. Let us realize, dear Sisters, that God is truly present here in this monastic chapel, where you have been gathering for many years at the times of prayer. From the altar, God, about whom we will be speaking, looks out on us and listens to us. If God so willed, he could achieve in us what he has achieved in certain of his saints. He could show himself to us in such a way that we could see him with our own eyes.

Although God remains shrouded in mystery, we can still acknowledge his presence with rapt adoration and intense love. In the wake of our adoration, while still savoring his living presence, we begin our conversation, knowing that God is now speaking to us.

The Blessed Virgin Mary is likewise with us. She rejoices that, during this week of retreat, we are striving to come to a keener knowledge and a loftier love of her son. Let us, the children of her household, implore Mary to incline our hearts and minds totally toward her son.

This evening, I would like, first of all, to make a special study of Christ, to place Christ before you as the object of your prayer, which is the essence of Carmel. We are vowed to prayer; it is the hallmark of our Order.

We did not come to Carmel to engage in intellectual studies, to have this or that particular activity (not even to direct a college!).[1]

We have come for one single reason: to pray, to be souls of prayer; that is to say, souls of love, who spend their lives loving God. And the rest, all the rest, whatever it may be, has no importance, absolutely no importance, whether it is an assignment at the turn, the kitchen, or any other office or function; nothing else exists in the eyes of God.

A passage I love very much from the Office of Lent is the responsorial that says: "Human beings see only the outside, the appearance, but God penetrates the heart" [1 Sam. 16:7]. Never does the gaze of God stop at the work of our hands and what we are engaged in doing. What matters for eternity is the heart with its intention of love. You recall the immensely profound saying of Saint John of the Cross: "In the evening of this life, we will be judged by love."[2] What a remarkable reversal of values will await us in heaven! God will look only at the heart, not at deeds, intelligence, or anything earthly. We will be judged by Love!

We are in Carmel only for this: to love! To love, of course, requires that we give proof of our love. This love expresses itself in constant prayer. I say "constant," because this state of prayer must be our life not for only two hours a day, but all day long. Our life must be a constant, silent prayer that rises unceasingly to God. That is what constitutes our duty in life.

We must not confuse this state of prayer with religious sentimentality, or with pious feelings unrelated to authentic prayer, which can sometimes be piercingly painful. That love, which is our life's duty, must express itself in vibrant, zealous deeds, all aspects of which compel our careful consideration.

Only with deepest humility can we recognize how far we are from our goal. Only those souls who have attained a lofty level of holiness can truly acknowledge how far they still are from their total fulfillment. For example, the Curé of Ars[3] considered himself more wretched than the notorious sinners to whom he ministered. He realized that many of these fallen souls, had they received the same graces that he had received, would perhaps surpass him in holiness. Only with humility can we recognize the torpor of our love.

Prayer is our primary duty. Prayer is the reason why God has placed us on earth. We learn truly to pray, when we are in the presence and company of Christ. Therefore, we must contemplate Christ for long periods of time and seek him out persistently. Consider those closest to Christ. Saint John the Apostle grasped what was indispensable for a clear understanding of his master. John never tired of probing and querying Christ. We can see how John thus gained richer insights and fuller explanations, precisely because he went to the bother of approaching and asking Christ to clarify each day's lesson. I picture John, walking close behind Christ, as he made his way about the Holy Land. Thus, John came to gain a wealth of intimate knowledge, which the other apostles did not acquire. Herein lies the explanation for the special character of the fourth Gospel. While the other apostles traveled across the then known world on their missionary journeys, John's unique apostolate was to remain close to the Virgin Mary, whom Christ had entrusted to him. Thus were these two great souls conjoined in love and prayer.

In Christ, all creation is subsumed. Christ enables us to see, to touch, and to hear God. Note how enthusiastically John expresses this truth in his Epistle: "... what we have heard, what we have seen with our eyes, what we have looked upon and touched with our hands...we proclaim now to you..." [1 Jn 1:13].

Let us now analyze the process whereby intellectual activity takes place in the human mind. A philosophical review of how we see, act, and grasp the mystery of things demonstrates that we must use our senses in order to develop our intelligence. We are well aware that there are some people who cannot see and others who cannot hear. Now, let us suppose that there were someone who had no external senses whatsoever, not even a sense of touch. That person's intelligence would remain a void. The soul needs the body as its intermediary in order to have the capacity to learn, to choose and to acquire all the elements of its intellectual life. Without the senses, our soul would have no images from which to draw its ideas. God is acutely aware of this fact.

There is an adage, which accurately states: "far from the eyes, far from the heart."[4] Conversely, we need to feel the presence of our beloved in order for the heart to be kept aflame and the relationship to be kept alive. After the loss of a loved one, little by little, the sorrow fades. To be sure, some remembrance remains, but it is not the same as when the person could be seen. So it is with nonbelievers. Unfortunately, they can neither see God nor find his presence in the Eucharist.

Therein lies the problem of why God willed the Incarnation. You are well aware of the great debate among medieval theologians concerning whether or not the Word of God would have become flesh, even if redemption were not necessary. One school of theologians was shocked to think that the Word of God would become flesh solely to overcome sin. They explicitly taught that, even in the absence of sin, the Word would have become flesh, because Christ alone was the adequate explanation for all creation. This vast universe with all its diverse forms of being would, they argued, have been created only in anticipation of the Incarnation.

A familiar, beautiful text from the Christmas liturgy of the hours describes the enthusiastic acclaim of the Word made flesh: "In the fullness of time, God sent his Son" [Gal. 4:4]. Then the heavens shook in admiration, for at the moment chosen by God from all eternity, the Word became flesh! This theological concept opens up vast horizons for us. This concept likewise explains the fall of the angels. For, God would ages ago have granted the angels a view of his Word made flesh and affirmed: "This Child is your King! You shall be his servants!" In this perspective, we come to understand the revolt of Lucifer, who was unwilling to serve this humble human being, and who, as a pure spirit, considered this corporeal being inferior to himself.

These vast theological horizons are worthy of deep meditation in prayerful silence. Despite the debate concerning whether God had anticipated the Incarnation independently of human sin or vice versa, it is nonetheless true that Christ is the way to reach, to touch, and to come to God. You are aware of how strongly Saint Teresa insisted that her Sisters faithfully follow Christ in order to find God. You are likewise aware of how often the vocations of countless great saints are rooted in the humanity of Christ. The divine and the human meet in marvelous mystery in Christ!

Saint Francis of Assisi experienced a vision in which Christ appeared to him and said: "Francis, will you please rebuild my church?" Francis set himself to work and came to realize that the Lord wished that the Church itself, not the chapel of San Damiano, be rebuilt.[5] (Saint Thérèse of the Child Jesus, gazing upon a picture of the bleeding hands of Christ, understood that the Lord's blood continues to be shed. She longed to collect this blood and to offer it to God for the salvation of the world.)[6] Countless others have likewise found the source of their vocations in the contemplation of Christ. Precisely because he is simultaneously God and man, Christ is paramount. He must be paramount for you, as the Scriptures confirm. There we read: "I am the way and the truth and the life. No one comes to the Father except through me" [Jn 14:6]. In their Letters, Saint Peter and Saint Paul consistently emphasize this theme: "Christ has given us an example in his life so that we can be examples in our lives."[7] Elsewhere Saint John tell us: "The Father loves the Son and has given everything over to him…we have seen his glory…and from his fullness we have all received, grace in place of grace…"[8] Saint Paul notes that in Christ "are hidden all the treasures of wisdom and knowledge" [Col. 2:3]. Finally, turning again to Saint John, we rediscover the reason for the Incarnation and for Christ's earthly mission: "You sent me into the world, my heavenly Father, so that men might see with their own eyes the light which you gave me before the creation of the world."[9]

You will undoubtedly be able to search out other similar texts in the sublime Gospel of Saint John and in the remarkable Letters of Saint Paul. In each instance you will surely see Saint John and Saint Paul stressing that we cannot come to God except through Christ.

There is a superb little book, which you may well know, *From Holy Communion to the Trinity*.[10] Its theme is that we advance from the bread to Christ and from Christ to the mystery of the Trinity. Christ is the center and the summation of God's plan. He enables us to discover God by using our bodily senses. The body is the instrument that makes God accessible to us. Let us, therefore, place ourselves at the feet of Christ in total tranquillity. Let us ask the Blessed Virgin Mary, Saint Teresa of Avila, Saint John of the Cross, and all the great saints who plumbed the mystery of Christ, to help us. In silent solitude, let us seek to discover the limitless love of God, revealed in Christ. Let us realize that we truly can be in contact with God. It is God whom we should aim to encounter in prayer. It is God who is both the breath and the fulfillment of our life. Amen.

Conference 3
To See Christ
Tuesday Morning

At Mass this morning, I read a Gospel story superbly suited to our retreat: the story of a rich man named Zacchaeus.[1] Because he was short in stature, despite his eagerness, he was unable to see Christ through the crowd. So Zacchaeus ran ahead and climbed up into a tree along the road where Christ was going to pass. Once he had seen Christ with his own eyes, he was determined to sell all that he had in order to help the poor. Then he said to the Lord: "If I have extorted anything from anyone, I shall repay it four times over" [Lk 19:8].

We cannot see Christ and remain as we are. We cannot exchange a look with Christ and not be overcome with a total conversion. If we are tepid and still attached to our ease, or if we do not have a total realization of the demands of our monastic vows, it is because we have not exchanged glances with Christ; we have not really "seen" Christ. This is what I would like to help you to do: to lead you to Christ so that you might, in the silence of retreat, exchange that glance with Christ; a true, living, and real contact that is not the fruit of the imagination, but rather reaches the heart of things as they are. Christ is a living being who is here, there, and everywhere. To see Christ, we must do as Zacchaeus did. We must become poor. Formerly, the weight of wealth overpowered him and prevented him from rising. Riches drag down the soul. One has to become small in stature, that is, detached from the goods of this world, for such riches foster earthly desires. As you are well aware, Saint John of the Cross warns: "Whether one is attached to earth by a silken thread or a gold cable, the result is the same: one cannot soar to the heights."[2] One attachment, however small, that violates our vows of obedience, poverty, or chastity, and draws us away from God, may be nothing by worldly standards. Nonetheless, that attachment comes between God and ourselves and impedes our ascent toward sanctity.

Ah, to see Christ! Each morning during Mass, we share the immense joy of the transformation of bread and wine into the Body and Blood of Christ. When we priests experience the wondrous joy of seeing the living Christ and touching him with our hands, I do not have to tell you our reaction. We want to close off the chapel and bow down in adoration before the Blessed Sacrament. There is an especially beautiful moment in the Mass, when the priest, as he holds the host, makes the sign of the cross three times over the chalice and twice between himself and the chalice. Then he raises the chalice and says: "per ipsum et cum ipso et in ipso..."[3] It is the living Christ through whom, with whom, and in whom, "all honor and glory is yours, almighty Father." It seems to me that at that precise moment, the priest shares in the omnipotence of God. At that precise moment our prayer has extraordinary efficacy, because the living Christ is as truly present as on Calvary. We climb toward God, as we pray wholeheartedly for the whole world, for our loved ones and for those requesting our remembrance.

Christ is all in all. Through him, all is made; through him, all comes to us. Therefore, we must see Christ. I stress this point: we must truly see Christ. I sometimes think that we should define the term Christian as "someone who has seen Christ." There are only a few genuine Christians, because only a few souls have seen Christ. Countless baptized persons, including even ordained priests and professed religious, remain lukewarm in spirit. Such tepid souls do not pulsate with life nor are they enthusiastic enough to give their life for Christ. They have never seen Christ. Their knowledge of the Lord is verbal, not vital. However, we must strive to love Christ passionately and prepare to see him face to face, when we die. The soul that neither misses Christ now nor longs to see him at life's end does not honestly love him. To make such a claim would be a lie. When we love someone, we long to see that person, even at the risk of death. All the more so, given his limitless love, we want to long to see Christ, face to face.

Let us now turn our attention to Saint John of the Cross. In his splendid writings, he explains how the person who loves God gradually pierces the veil that keeps us from seeing the Lord. Eventually, the moment comes, when that veil is totally sundered and the person goes forth to our beloved God.

When I speak of persons who have seen Christ, I am not referring to the type of vision often recorded in the lives of such saints
When I speak of seeing Christ, I
sion of faith, which is the fruit of
id not the result of any activity on
ce of being "swept up" by Christ
ntly devoted ourselves to charity,
control, and when Christ has seen
nent, then he himself comes to us.
veloped in the divine being and
nce of God himself. We know that
o us, but not in words. The human

heart communicates directly with the heart of Christ in the blissful adoration of simple regard. This heartfelt vision of Christ compels the soul so to love Christ and so to make him loved that nothing else on earth can inspire greater love than the Lord. Wealth then is as nothing and poverty is prized precisely because it allows us greater intimacy with Christ. No other comfort, no other countenance and no other solace suffices. Christ alone provides satisfaction.

When our spiritual father Saint John of the Cross speaks of the "dark night of the soul,"[6] he is describing the disappearance of the conscious sense of God's presence from the soul, which must then rely solely on the dim light of faith. That soul is plunged into spiritual aridity, incapable of loving anything earthly. Such a soul can be satisfied only by the love of God, but that love seems to have vanished. Nothing can be seen. Nothing remains except faith, separation, and abandonment. This is a terrible trial. However, this trial can bring renewed strength to the soul, as it waits for its Beloved once again to allow himself to be seen. This singularly meritorious trial enables the soul to leap forward into the embrace of God and thus to live in intimacy with Christ.

How glorious is this intimacy with Christ! This intimacy yields an inexhaustible source of contemplation and a continuous unfolding of the great mystery of Christ's Incarnation. We see Christ in all stages of his human development. We see him being formed in the womb of his Mother. We see him as an infant or as a little boy. We see him as an adolescent in the midst of the teachers in the Temple or as an apprentice at work in Nazareth, earning his wages by the sweat of his brow. We see him as a grown man at the outset of his apostolic life or at its end, as he hangs upon the cross. Therein, we find the roots of contemplation. Therein, we find a person just like us, as he walks and talks, as he eats and sleeps, as he grows tired and sits by the well, as he weeps and suffers. That person is God himself here with us.

When the Virgin Mary hugged her newborn son, it was Christ the Lord whom she held in her arms. What a sublime consolation for Mary! When the Apostles looked at their Master and spoke with him, the person before them was Christ the Lord. There we encounter the marvelous mystery of Christ. He is the God-Man, yet he does not have a human personality. Rather, it is the infinite person of God in whom Christ subsists, and through whom Christ is made incarnate.

What a magnificent mystery is revealed in the Incarnation of the Word! In the human person are found both a spiritual soul and a material body. In the soul, there are two dominant faculties, intelligence and will. In turn, the will is identified with the heart, which is the seat of both love and the emotions. But beyond even the soul there is the human person, in whom these two elements, the spiritual and the material, are conjoined. Philosophers strain to grasp the subtle nature of the human person. Even when there is agreement on the existence of human nature, it is difficult to define its properties.

In analyzing ourselves, each one of us readily realizes our own personhood. This irreducible "me" embodies the best in each one of us. This "me" remains despite all the upheavals and changes in our lives. Throughout all our joys and sorrows, in health and in sickness, our human personality presides over every stage of life, from cradle to grave. That personality embraces our memories and our fantasies as well as our pride and our shame at various times in our lives. That personality enables us to pray, to love, and to act be it basely or bravely. It is this mysterious "me" which imparts all value to our being. An animal acts instinctively, without any awareness of life's beauty. By contrast, the human personality is destined for eternal life and thirsts for the truest, purest, loftiest happiness possible.

When we scrutinize Christ, we find in him, an authentic human nature composed of both a real body and a real soul with all its faculties. As his intellect developed, Christ acquired language and discovered the marvels of nature. We find in him also a will with a loving heart and a spirit capable of prayerful knowledge of God. That spirit was likewise capable of suffering the intense pain of the dark night of the soul, as when he cried out from the cross, "Eloi, Eloi, lema sabachthani?" [Mk 15:34].[7] However, what we do not find in Christ is that overarching human "me." Therein, we confront a majestic mystery. It is the very person of the Word of God that brings to completion and accounts for the acts of Christ's human nature.

From the first moment of his conception by the Holy Spirit in the womb of the Virgin Mary, the Word of God conferred the finishing touch on existing human nature, as only a divine person could. As a result, whatever Christ did through his human nature derived from a divine person and thus acquired its full value. Although the acts of Christ were physically human, they were nonetheless truly divine. For us as humans, all our actions bear the imprint of our intentions and our character. For Christ, the case is different. The human nature of the Word of God endows his actions with such infinite merit that it is no exaggeration to say that Christ would have needed to live for just a few seconds in order to redeem the world.

What a rapturous reflection the Virgin Mary experienced, when she first gazed into the eyes of her infant son and there discovered a glint of God's infinity!

I leave you with these thoughts on the intimate nature of Christ. Immerse yourselves in total silence during this retreat. Gaze upon Christ, as did the Virgin Mary. Thus you will come to see him with the eyes of your soul. Let your love for him be total!

Let your life be transformed by this constantly burning desire to be willing to die in order to see Christ face to face. Amen.

Conference 4
Christ at Prayer
Tuesday Evening

We are going to make our prayer this evening, in the presence of the Blessed Virgin Mary. We have been striving for a fuller knowledge of her Son. However, we must do so in her presence. From now until tomorrow evening, we will place ourselves in intimate union with Mary, whose feast we celebrate.[1] To do otherwise, would be to act irreverently.

So, placing ourselves in Mary's presence, let us live these twenty-four hours of her feast in intimate union with our Blessed Mother. She is so sweet, so gentle, and so eager to help us in our spiritual life, even if, as is often the case, we do not listen attentively to her voice. Let us tenderly ask Mary, who is here with us and pleased by our awareness of her presence, to help us to pray more intensely than ever before.

I would like to join with you in observing Christ at prayer. On occasion, his apostles observed Christ at prayer, perhaps at sunset or after the last of the sick and the curious headed home. Then, when the weary apostles searched for lodgings and longed for rest at the end of the day, Christ sought solitude, usually on the top of a hill, looking out toward the distant horizon. There he remained for some time, absorbed in prayer.[2] What was his prayer like? Our conference this evening can help us answer that question.

Have you ever wondered what Christ's prayer was like? Upon examination, we realize that his prayer consisted essentially in the penetration of his very being by God. Consider the experience of Saint John of the Cross. His life was brief, because his great love prepared him for an early death. Near the end of his life, he tells us how at Beas,[3] he could not hear the name of God uttered without entering into ecstasy. His body lost its weight and rose toward heaven. It was as if he were caught up and carried off by the movement of his soul in its eagerness to head off to God. The Lord truly dwelled within him.

I vividly remember a priest in Le Havre. Whenever I would go very early in the morning to offer Mass at his church, he was already there, deep in prayer. I was struck by the fact that, when I approached him, he seemed to take a break from his conversation with God. It was as if he were saying: "Please, excuse me, Lord. I have to help someone. I'll be back as soon as possible." That priest gave the impression of being fully absorbed in the presence of God. Our prayer should reach that level of intensity and development. Then, there would be no need to regard coming to chapel twice a day to pray or having to kneel in adoration at certain times as requirements of our Rule.[4] Rather, prayer should be our steady, supernatural method of breathing, day and night, in the silence of our souls. Our prayer should grow more intense at certain times and those times should increase in both frequency and duration. Eventually, even daily duties in the kitchen will be subsumed into prayer, and nothing will be able to disrupt its focus. Neither changes within the community nor disorderly crowds outside in the streets, not even the whistles of passing trains will be able to shatter our state of prayer.

The prayer of the saints, especially of our blessed Father, Elijah, is simultaneously profound, persevering and within reach. By way of contrast, Saint John of the Cross had to restrain himself in order not to become too profoundly absorbed in prayer. He sought to mortify himself severely in order to keep his soul within his body and thus prevent it from being swallowed up in loving contemplation of God.

That spiritual state should be our quest and goal. Bear in mind the words of Saint John of the Cross: "It is not God who fails our souls; it is our souls that fail God."[5] When God seeks to test the perseverance of the soul through suffering or trials, through disappointments or challenges, consider the outcome. Many souls, who longed to taste the sweetness of prayer, but not to have direct contact with God for his own sake, take flight. In the words of the familiar saying, they longed to taste "the consolations of God, but not the God of all consolations." In truth, are we any different? Are we not likewise lacking in courage and total acceptance? Do we not seek to exercise choice, to impose conditions, and to make bargains in our relationship with God? By contrast, Saint Thérèse of the Child Jesus said: "I accept all."[6] "Yes, Lord, I accept all," meant for her: I accept being as I am and remaining as you wish, provided that I find you and live ever more closely with you.

This quick glance at the prayer of the saints lets us discover the tremendous depth of the prayer of Christ. Prayer involves penetration by God. However, as we have already noted, the very being of Christ entails a human nature subsisting in the divine persons, inseparably united as one and the same God. Thus the divine persons are not three detached beings, but rather are the one God, infinite in being. As a result, wherever the Word is, there too is the Father and there too is the Holy Spirit.

Our very limited human mind is overwhelmed by this unfathomable mystery. However, our mind can still understand that there is something in God that surpasses human nature. The human heart of Christ grasped God fully, not partially through the veil of faith, as we do.

By virtue of the hypostatic union, Christ sees God directly, with no veil of separation. The expression "hypostatic union" means the union of a human nature subsisting in a divine personality or "self." Hence, from the very first moment that the Word became flesh, Christ possessed the beatific vision, which we can know only in heaven. Christ had this direct, unmediated vision of God every moment of his life. In Christ the penetration of God is total and unlimited.

With us, even when called by God to the highest levels of prayer, as in the case of the saints and even of the Blessed Virgin Mary, there remains a screen, a human person. When God comes to penetrate that person, he limits his penetration, by allowing that person to live on. God cannot give himself to that person in all his infinite fullness. In sharp contrast, however, Christ sees God with complete clarity and awareness.

How boundless and constant is Christ's prayer! Throughout his life, Christ beholds God, as we will do in heaven. Yet, that vision does not prevent Christ from acting in accordance with his human nature. He develops his faculties and learns to say "Daddy" and "Mama," at the same pace as other children. He works with his hands and earns his livelihood by the sweat of his brow. Later on, he watches out for his family and his apostles, making sure that they have food to eat. He fulfills all his daily duties. However, these practical tasks never impinge upon his profound prayer. Whether he is planing planks at work or going to school or doing errands for his mother, he is uninterruptedly engaged in deep prayer.

Those who maintain that basic duties, social service, physical labor, or intellectual activity can interrupt prayer are mistaken. Recall the episode in the life of Saint Thérèse of the Child Jesus, when she was in her room sewing. One of the novices came along unexpectedly and was struck by the radiant beauty of her face. The novice asked: "What are you pondering, Sister?" Saint Thérèse replied unassumingly: "I was just meditating on the Pater Noster and reflecting on how beautiful it is to say 'Our Father,' when speaking to God."[7] Her hands were at work, but her heart was at prayer. Bear in mind, her state of prayer was the same, even in the laundry.

No work can interrupt prayer. The example of both Christ and the saints confirms this point. What a major mistake it would be to think that prayer can be offered only in the silence of the chapel or, conversely, that prayer cannot be made in the whole range of human activities. Prayer consists in the contemplation of God and requires only that we open ourselves up to penetration by God. Since Christ enjoys the beatific vision, we want to consider his state of unceasing prayer. If we examine the Gospel, we see Christ concerned about one thing above all: to do the will of God. Christ is so absorbed in God and God so suffuses every cell of Christ that there is no point where the whims of human nature can divert Christ from God. In God, being and will are infinitely identical.

We are the ones who make distinctions in our study of God. We need to make distinctions precisely because we are not simple. God, however, is simple, not because of any lack of perfection, but rather because of the infinite richness of his being. His simplicity is complete, because his will is his very self; that is, God willing. For God's will is not a faculty distinct from his divine substance. As we know from our own spiritual life, such is not the case with us. In turn, we see that Christ has only one goal. In his life and work, Christ's sole aim is to conform himself completely to God's will and thus to make God known.

Christ himself tells us this truth in the Gospels. For example, we read in the Gospel of John: "My food is to do the will of the one who sent me" [Jn 4:34]. Turning to the Gospel of Matthew, we find: "not the smallest letter or the smallest part of a letter will pass from the law until all things have taken place" [Mt 5:18]. Moreover, in the Gospel of John, we read: "I do not seek to do my own will, but the will of the one who sent me" [Jn 5:30]; and again: "the Father who sent me commanded me what to say and speak" [Jn 12:4]. Then, at the end of his life, the full realization of the enormity of his Passion became clear to Christ. You can be sure that Christ was in no way impervious to the stupendous suffering set out before him. In fact, he recoiled at the prospect. His human nature shuddered in fear. He was so stricken that he began to sweat blood and cried out: "Father, if you are willing, take this cup away from me; still, not my will but yours be done" [Lk 22:42]. Finally, when the cup had been emptied and all his blood had gushed out from his countless wounds, Christ turned toward his father and said: "It is finished. And bowing his head, he handed over the spirit" [Jn 19:30].

Here then, dear Sisters, is the fruit of Christ's prayer. Because he contemplates as any other human being, and because his prayer is a constant heart-to-heart communication with God or, more precisely, a dwelling in God, it is a total and immensely heroic obedience. He has one care only: to obey God. He is rooted in obedience as faithfully as he is rooted in prayer.

We follow the opposite path. Christ started out from contemplation to come to the perfection of obedience. We must start out from the perfection of obedience to arrive at contemplation. This is the reverse route we must follow. In the depths of our being, our prayer is worth what our obedience is worth. Our embrace of God will be in accordance with our embrace of his will.

Whatever brings us to this point be it a superior or a sorrow, a sickness or a job, it is always God who comes and speaks to us. When we embrace obedience, we embrace God. When we obey with a smile, we smile at God and welcome him joyfully into our home. To dream of profound prayer, like that of the saints, while withholding the obedience of the saints, is a contradiction.

Let us examine the achievement of Saint John of the Cross and his humble obedience, regardless of the circumstances. Let us listen to his prayer, when Christ said to him: "John, John, what do you ask of me?" And, John, with his deep appreciation of the cross, replied: "Lord, let me be unrecognized and despised for love of you." He made this prayer to his friend Christ and his prayer was heard.[8] Christ certainly gave him several signs of his affection. Yet, in his final hours, John was covered with sores from head to toe and languished under the authority of a hard-hearted prior. Is this not a lesson for us, the spiritual sons and daughters of Saint John of the Cross, concerning the remarkably rich benefits of humble obedience, especially in distressing circumstances?

Let us consider, then, what constituted this profound prayer in the soul of Christ. Let us contemplate the great mysteries of the beatific vision and the hypostatic union. Let us go to work courageously to welcome God within us, so that we can know the immense nourishment to be derived from constant, deep prayer. We will reach out for this prayer with humility and obedience.

To understand the happiness of the presence of God and to have a foretaste of heaven here below, let us take the necessary steps, while repeating the words found in our Office: "Taste and see the goodness of the Lord" [Ps. 34:9]. May we experience the truth of his words and may we likewise know the road that leads to him. Amen.

Conference 5
The Divine Preparation in Mary and in Us
Wednesday Morning

Yesterday, on the anniversary of the dedication of your chapel, dear Sisters, the Office was especially beautiful. This week you have read exquisite texts. There is one of those texts that I am eager to explore with you this morning. That text concerns the Virgin Mary, whose feast is celebrated today in every city throughout the Catholic world,[1] and reads: "How awesome is this place! This is none other than the house of God; this is the gate of heaven."[2] That spot, that place, that little corner of creation induces a respectful fear of the Lord, because it is the house of God and the gate that opens out to heaven.

You are correct in thinking that these liturgical texts presented for our meditation concern much more than a dwelling place made of stone. These texts are addressed to us and need to be applied to the Blessed Virgin Mary, who fulfilled every dimension of the spiritual life. Thus, it is totally proper to say of her: "This is the house of God and the gate of heaven."

These words should likewise apply to us. However, so far as we are concerned, other terms need to be used. You recall how Our Lord spoke to the merchants in the Temple and to the guards assigned to protect the Temple from worldly profanation. He exclaimed: "My house shall be a house of prayer, but you are making it a den of thieves" [Mt 21:13]. Christ could likewise direct this reproach at us. If we are totally truthful, we should reproach ourselves in these very terms. We are poor sinners, who fail to show tenderness to our friend, the Lord. We are false and fickle friends. Our union with Christ is such that we are called "spouses of the Word."[3] But we are unfaithful spouses and unwise virgins, who let our lamps burn out. The uproar within our souls and the turbulence of our memories, as well as our yearnings, transform us from being peaceful points of prayer into boisterous, disorderly market places. That is what we really are. However, the Blessed Virgin Mary is truly a house of prayer and truly a dwelling place of God. Let us turn our attention to this beautiful creation of God.

I urge each of you to reread privately in the course of the day the splendid first reading from today's Mass. It is drawn from the Book of Wisdom.[4] The Church applies to the Blessed Virgin Mary what is said therein concerning the Wisdom of God. This passage tends to confirm the theological position to which I referred earlier. According to one influential school of thought, the Word would have become flesh, even if there had been no original sin. Because he is the fullness of all creation, and because the immense universe was brought into existence by the infinite power of God, there is need of no other creative purpose than to prepare for the Incarnation of the Word. The epistle[5] [from today's Mass] appears to support that position. There we read regarding the Blessed Virgin Mary, the Mother of Christ: "The Lord begot me, the first-born of his ways, the forerunner of his prodigies of long ago… before the mountains were settled into place, before the hills, I was brought forth… Then was I beside him as his craftsman, and I was his delight day by day. Playing before him all the while…"[6] That text tends to indicate the pre-existence in God's thought of the one chosen to be the Mother of the Word made flesh. Therefore, before every other consideration, there is special concern for the creation of the woman who would fashion a human body for the Word made flesh. There is no need for me to emphasize to you the markedly different concluding lines of the epistle: "Happy the man who obeys me and happy those who keep my ways; happy the man watching daily at my gates, waiting at the doorposts; for he who finds me finds life and wins favor from the Lord" [Prov. 8:3-35].

Thus, the Blessed Virgin Mary, as the mediatrix of all graces and the source of all life, was of special concern in God's preparation for the Incarnation. She was a prime presence in God's plan, as he contemplated the creation of the universe in preparation for the Incarnation of the Son.

This morning we want to turn our attention to the deep inner beauty of Mary's life. In his discussion of the preparations required in order for Mary to be the worthy mother of Christ, Father Monsabré used an excellent expression. He said: "In his divine preparations, God plays the grand organ."[7] Previously, God had created a wide array of human beings, including great prophets and patriarchs. He had extended his creative hand over the surface of the world, leaving upon the earth the dazzling imprint of his own brilliant beauty. That is the beauty the Psalmist calls to mind each day when we pray: "Bless the Lord, all you works of the Lord."[8] Indeed, we recognize the imprint of God's beauty in the flowers and the sunlight, in the colors of the rainbow and the whistle of the wind. We recognize that beauty in every enchantment of nature. However, all that beauty pales in comparison to Mary. As a little girl, Mary drew no special notice and was regarded as no different from other children. Yet, this simple little girl had a very special calling; she was to be the mother of God.

I am going to digress at this point to note that certain leading heretics in the early Christian centuries disputed the title "Mother of God." They argued that one could not speak of the "Mother of God." They held that the Virgin Mary gave Christ only his body. Therefore, she was the mother of the human person, but not of God. However, the Church correctly responded to Nestorius[9] and his followers that, when a human mother conceives a child, she gives her child its body, but not its soul. That soul is created directly by God. Thus, the mother fashions the child's flesh and God himself infuses the soul, which makes the child a human being and not just an animal.

To be sure, the Virgin Mary did not give Christ his divine nature. Nevertheless, she is the mother of the whole person. So it is with us. We do not say of our mothers that they are mothers of our bodies, but not of our souls. We say that they are the mothers of their children and mothers of "us." Hence, the Virgin Mary is truly the mother of Christ and, since his human nature subsists in the divine person, Mary is likewise truly the mother of God. Jesus clearly demonstrated his sense of respectful submission to his parents: "He went down with them and came to Nazareth, and was obedient to them" [Lk 3:5]. The woman whose praises we will be singing throughout this day is the Mother of God. We will express our prayerful admiration in the poetic words of the Office: "For you carried in your womb, the One whom the heavens cannot contain."[10]

It is so awesome that it makes us weep with admiration and thanksgiving to think that a poor little human creature, our sister human being, had the tremendous honor of forming a body and bringing God into the world. She received him, she guarded him, she enclosed him in the humble, narrow limits of her own body. What a privilege! The creator of the world called her "Mama." She held him in her arms and cradled him at her breast. You know very well that creation was not a passing gesture, as if God had withdrawn, leaving his work to continue according to determined laws. Creation is actually continuing while I speak to you. If God discontinued his creating action, all beings would instantly return to nothingness. Creation is a work that continues unceasingly. This is a consoling thought, which puts us in the presence of God and into contact with the being of God. Thus the little one who was there under Mary's eyes was continuing the act of creating the world; he was creating and maintaining his mother in existence.

You may well imagine that such an exceptional creature should be full of grace in order to accomplish her sublime role, and rightly so. God always prepares the being to whom he would confide a great mission. Each one of us has been and will remain chosen by God. He has given us a special mission to be the saviors of the world. Because we have this mission, we are chosen before others for his service of love, and have received particular divine preparation. It is essential for us to realize this truth in order not to disappoint God by wasting his gift or by nullifying his special divine preparations. Let us do as the Virgin Mary did. When the moment arrived, the angel came to reveal God's plan, saying: "Do you wish to accept the role of mother of the savior of the world?" She replied: *"Fiat"* [let it be done]. She knew neither how this could take place nor how she would be able to reconcile it with her vow [of virginity]. Still she surrendered herself to God's will for her. And what do we do? What have we done with God's preparations in us? When something disconcerting happens to us, do we say *"fiat"* so that the divine plan may not be squandered or lessened in its efficacy? We should be saints and allow the divine plan to be fulfilled to its utmost extent. Alas! Where do we stand?

For the Virgin Mary, God's preparation consisted of the fullness of grace that she received in her Immaculate Conception. In order for Mary to be completely free from sin, she had to be totally open to God's will. You are familiar with the writings of Saint Alphonsus of Ligouri.[11] In his explanation, by virtue of the Immaculate Conception, the Virgin Mary received not merely the negative privilege of freedom from sin, but more importantly the positive privilege of habitual grace. Her endowment exceeded the graces of all the other saints combined. Her graces multiplied and became torrents overflowing her soul.

Divine preparations are always and above all spiritual rather than material. Consider this woman, destined to bring into the world the One who surpasses all human expectations. Consider how God stripped this woman of all material riches. Although she is of royal ancestry, God wills the mother of his Son to be a simple worker from a worker's family. He strips her of luxury and social standing. Paradoxically, the very poor woman who gives birth to the Son is the paragon of true wealth. Again and again we encounter the same lesson: in order to find the fullness of God, we must hold on to nothing, absolutely nothing. Our fingers and hands must be free. In order for God to penetrate our lives, we must separate ourselves from everything else. So it was with the Virgin Mary. God alone dwelled in the depths of her soul. A stupendous surge of supernatural grace swelled within her and made her worthy to be the mother of the Word made flesh.

As we meditate on the soul of the Virgin Mary, as we return to yesterday's first reading, and as we reflect on the striking words of the Office, we want to gaze upon the young girl who came into the world, prepared by God to be his mother. This evening we observe her at prayer. The secret of her prayer is her complete conformity to God's preparations within her. We must likewise consider God's preparations within us, since we are called to bring God to others. Let us ask God to help us remain faithful, so that, when the moment of our special mission does come, we will be totally ready to say: *"Fiat, fiat mihi secundum Verbum tuum!"* [12] Amen.

Conference 6
Virginity in God and in Mary
Wednesday Evening

For a moment, let us focus our full attention on the living presence of God and consciously consider our closeness to him. Let us also link ourselves with the Virgin Mary, whom we solemnly honor today on the feast of Our Lady of Pontoise.[1] Again this evening we are going to consider the Virgin Mary.

It seems to me that Christ wants us to note that he chose to be born of a virgin. It is this specific characteristic, which we observe in the Virgin Mary as the Mother of Christ, that I wish to examine with you this evening. In the light of this examination, we will be better able to plumb the depths of the heart and soul of the Virgin Mary. Thus, we will come to discover certain aspects of her life of prayer.

The Mother of Christ is a virgin. When God took on human form, he wanted to assure this characteristic in his mother. By virtue of our vow of chastity, it is essential for us to make this commitment shine forth, even if contemporary culture does not grasp its full meaning. Because we have made vows of chastity, we are designated as virgins. This characteristic is one of the crown jewels of Mary's divine motherhood. That same terminology is often applied to us. Perhaps we deceive ourselves by narrowing this beautiful concept. I am afraid that you yourselves do not always see how this beautiful title applies to your life of sacrifice. I am afraid that you regard chastity only in terms of the absence of sensual gratification. Virginity, however, is a very different matter.

Let us now fix our gaze on the bosom of God and the mystery of the Trinity, to the degree that revelation permits. I maintain that the Word of God is total, absolute virginity. Here is the reason why. As you are well aware, there is in the inner life of the Trinity a stupendous cycle, which overwhelms our poor, little minds. The pure intelligence of God conceives the being itself of God. The divine intelligence grasps and sees itself; it speaks and expresses itself. It grasps and expresses itself in a word, which equals the intelligence that sets it forth. With infinite simplicity, the divine nature eternally expresses the Word of God. In this one word is the infinite activity of the divine intelligence. The Word of God, begotten by the Father, is the infinite, equal, and divine expression of the very Being of God. The Word possesses the fullness of the divine nature, just as does the Father, and thus is truly God. In the infinite simplicity of God's being, this unfathomable, living expression shines forth so brilliantly that a third person, an outpouring of love, unites in a single nature this Word and the One who begets him from all eternity.

These three persons: the Father, the Son begotten by the Father, and the Holy Spirit, whose infinite breath of love unites the three, constitute the perfect purity of God. That divine purity is what I term the fullness of virginity. Such is God himself!

In Christ, as we saw the other day, there is something sublime in the realization of virginity. The human nature given in its totality to the Word is divinized in every respect. Therein, the gift of self to God attains its greatest conceivable realization. Christ, as a human being without a trace of vacillation and with unimaginable integrity, brings to admirable fulfillment his mission of total virginity.

We have also seen God's remarkable preparation of the Virgin Mary for her role as Mother of the Word made flesh. God exempted her from original sin and its consequences. Thus, in the Virgin Mary, there comes about the restoration of what had been destroyed by Adam's sin, especially the reestablishment of the proper balance between the natural and the supernatural. At the time of their creation by God, Adam and Eve were endowed with a perfectly ordered constitution. The body carried out all its natural activities in an orderly, peaceful way. Just as the body worked in total submission to its spiritual faculties, so the soul carried out all its activities in total submission to God, its master. Adam and Eve came into existence and continued in existence with total dependence on God. As creatures, they were necessarily beings who did not exist of and by themselves.

God is his own reason for being; he has not drawn his existence from anything else. "God is" and "I Am Who am" [cf. Ex 3:14] are rich phrases that contemplative religious relish.

God is pure act, as the philosophers say; that is, he is the total realization of all possibility. We are not pure act; we have not realized all possibilities of being that are in us. Our being evolves as our heart intensifies its affections and perfects them. Our body grows and then declines. God himself is pure actuality, pure act. Nothing in him is in the state of possibility, passing from nonexistence to existence. All is infinite existence in him.

The human person, on the contrary, far from being this totality of realization, is a creature of infirmity and dependence. Remember what I was saying to you regarding creation? Nothing exists that cannot be annihilated instantly, if the creative action ceases to operate. It is this way, because we are not self-existent beings, as the words of Our Lord to Saint Catherine of Siena indicated: "You are she who is not."[2] This is the foundation of our being. We are not; we have only a borrowed being, unceasingly renewed by God. The Virgin Mary shares this condition of creaturehood with us. By herself she was not; she was totally dependent, as we are totally dependent.

It is precisely this quality that constitutes the Virgin Mary's virginity. She is pure creature; God is pure deity, totally independent. For the Virgin Mary, her virginity lies in being a pure creature of God, namely, a creature living in that total dependence on the will of God. Indeed, when we examine the Virgin Mary's life, when we gather the conclusions of the Fathers of the Church who dwelt on this Marian mystery, and when we study the works of theologians, we find that she was absolutely obedient to the will of God, even to the least indications of that will. The virginity of the Virgin Mary is founded on her pure dependence on God.

When the angel Gabriel came to ask Mary's consent to the unique honor and extravagant joy of being the Mother of God, the Lord did not issue an order. Instead, he asks, "Will you?" This singular honor was proposed only to Mary, one woman among the millions God created. In this example, we discern a pattern of action observed by God in regard to all souls. God exercises a mind-boggling respect for every soul. He respects our freedom more than we ourselves do. He respects the secrets and the mindset of each person in a way we cannot match.

God asks this young woman: "Will you be the Mother of the Word who is going to take flesh?" What a radical turn of events for this young woman! The thought of becoming a mother completely changed every aspect of her future, as she had anticipated it. However, as soon as she realized that this message came from God, her creator and master, she replied at once, in words reflecting her total contingency, *"Ecce ancilla Domini."*[3] I have nothing else to say to my master. Years later, you recall, her son stayed at the Temple and she anxiously searched for him. Upon finding him, she exclaimed, as any mother would have: "Son, why have you done this to us?" [Lk 2:48]. Jesus responded: "Why were you looking for me? Did you not know that I must be in my Father's house?" [Lk 2:49]. Thus, when he was twelve years old and just entering adulthood, Jesus began to indicate that he had come into the world to establish the reign of God in human hearts. Again, Mary remained silent. She accepted everything, regardless of the consequences for her own motherly heart.

Let us gaze upon Mary especially during the tragic hours of the Passion. You will not see her dramatically displaying her sorrow, as many mothers would. The Virgin Mary is there, walking along with her son and sharing all his sorrow, but utters not a word, not a rebuke, not a plea aimed at diminishing the suffering she sees. She totally embraces the will of God, as it unfolds in the brutal treatment of her child. She acts in complete accord with her role as a creature and does not try to alter the divine plan. She is a creature, pure and simple; she is a virgin. Although time does not permit us to dwell on the point, this virginity and this characteristic of a pure creature, grounded in obedience, is Mary's special grace of prayer.

Habitual grace flooded Mary's soul and made her conscious of her condition as creature and shaped her as a virgin, eager to obey the will of God alone. This fidelity, in turn, increases her merit and occasions a further outpouring of grace. Thus comes about an extraordinary cycle. Mary's virginity wins her new graces, which enable her ever more consciously to realize her role as a total virgin.

We will likewise be virgins to the degree that we are faithful to our role as creatures. In that perspective, virginity consists not merely of the absence of sensual pleasures and feelings but also of something far greater. Virginity entails eliminating within us any thing that does not come from God and does not express God's will.

Let us strive for that goal. Let us see if we are worthy of the lofty title of virgin. That title is reserved for the soul who valiantly and totally submits to God, as did the Blessed Virgin Mary. Amen.

Conference 7
Our Three Vows: Total Death
Thursday Morning

During a retreat, we should strive, not with our minds but primarily with our hearts, to listen to the priest who is interpreting God's thoughts and plans for us. Our conferences are not scholarly seminars. Rather, they are prayers, which we offer together. At each conference, we should come together in God's presence, placing ourselves at Christ's feet and acknowledging that the Lord has brought us together. Remember that Christ is here present and remember, too, the countless number of persons who live, almost as animals, without any awareness of God in their midst.

Recall the words Christ spoke to Saint Margaret Mary: "Behold this Heart which has so loved men and is so little loved in return! You, at least, love me."[1] Let us, at least, not live a life devoid of God's presence, as do pagans. Let us remain always close to God, as he gazes down on us. Let us place ourselves in his living presence.

This morning, in intimate union with the Lord, I would like you to join with me in meditating on the role of our vows in our prayer and in our spiritual life. We have already considered how Christ is a divine, but not a human person. We have also considered how the Blessed Virgin Mary actualized her virginity by being a creature in the fullest sense of the term. Christ possessed the beatific vision precisely because no human "I" separated him from God. Thus Christ directly beheld God's very being, as seen in heaven. Christ lived and moved about, bearing heaven within himself.

Conversely, the Blessed Virgin Mary did have a human "I." As a totally human creature, she was a human person. As such, she would say, "I wish, I love or I do," on the basis of her human personhood, which informed all her human actions. However, the Virgin Mary was so closely conformed to God's will, that her human "I" dissolved and became bathed in the divine will. Thus, both Christ and Mary attained the pinnacle of prayer. Such prayer is the goal of the entire teaching of Saint John of the Cross. It is the "Living Flame of Love," which blazes at the summit of the road and crowns the conclusion of the canticle. It is Mount Carmel itself.[2] That flame burns with infinite intensity in Christ and with brilliant brightness in the Virgin Mary. Like all others who have come to Carmel, we have come with that same goal in mind. *"A[d] quid venisti?"*[3]

In response to the question: what is our life's work, we have said: to be persons of prayer. If we are not persons of prayer, our lives are meaningless. Even God can do nothing with us, if we are not persons of prayer. In the words of the Gospel: "You are the salt of the earth. But, if salt loses its taste, with what can it be seasoned? It is no longer good for anything, but to be thrown out and trampled underfoot" [Mt 5, 13]. In both the Church on earth and the Kingdom of Heaven, we are useless, unless we are persons of prayer. We live our life only once, not twice. Therefore, each day, which slips slowly through our fingers, hour by hour, is irretrievable. A life misspent is lost forever. Our life is a failure, if it is not a life of contemplation, love, and prayer.

In Christ and in the Virgin Mary, the action of God himself slew, so to speak, in a single stroke, the human "I." In them, anything potentially opposed to God's plan, and so to God himself, was expunged. Christ had no need of human personhood. Since Christ is definitively divine, it is completely impossible for him to have even the least imperfection. Recall what I said earlier: "One cannot see God and sin." For that very reason, the blessed in heaven are grounded in goodness. If Adam and Eve had gazed upon God in the beatific vision, they would never have committed their sin. Despite their abundant graces, they did not see God with their own eyes. They, like us, saw only through faith.

In Christ, as in the Virgin Mary, God's direct, unique intervention brought about their life of profound prayer, which transcended anything human in them. There was, then, not the slightest imperfection in them that could turn their will away from God. Such a death is equally essential for us. We must die to ourselves. Our "I" must come to know this mystical death in order to attain a life of profound prayer. To the degree that we die to ourselves, to that degree will we come to know the fullness of prayer. There truly is a direct correlation between mystical death and the full flowering of prayer. Let us keep in mind the words of Christ: if the grain of wheat does not fall into the ground and die, it remains just a grain of wheat; but, if it falls into the ground and lets itself die, then it becomes transformed and yields fruit a hundredfold.[4]

So it is with us. If we hold on to ourselves for fear of mystical death and the surrender of our worldly desires, and if we hold on to our soul with its earthly attitudes, then we will remain just as we are with our own little soul and our own little bit of human happiness. In order to grow rich in God and all that comes from God, we must die to ourselves. We must let our human "I" diminish and ultimately coalesce into the divine will, the very being of God.

This mystical death is directly achieved through our vows. On the day of our solemn profession, we gather up, as it were, all that we are and all that we have. Then, in a single stroke, we make all that disappear, by offering everything to God. This death is so real that throughout our life the effects of our solemn profession are comparable to those of Baptism. In Baptism, our fallen nature disappears along with all its faults, imperfections, and burdens. A new being thus comes to life, bearing the imprint of heaven and the Holy Trinity. In fact, if the newly baptized person dropped dead, that person would go directly to heaven, regardless of past actions.

Solemn profession produces a similar outcome. If the soul were separated from the body on profession day, it would go directly to heaven. That soul's past, along with its human "I," has disappeared. The person who has just made solemn profession is a new creation, transformed by God's presence. This mystical death affects every aspect of our life. Consider the effect of poverty. Every human person seeks reassurance regarding the future. We all feel that we are destined for something great and enduring. But even that is not enough for us. We feel impelled to go still further and reach for the stars. Those who aim to amass great fortunes, are responding to that basic instinct of wanting something noteworthy and enduring. However, they are clearly mistaken in thinking that material possessions will satisfy their souls. Ultimately, the only source of inner peace and the actual attainment of the heart's deepest desires is increased participation in God's infinity.

The soul is made to possess infinity, a spiritual infinity, God's Infinity. Therefore, material goods can never satisfy the soul. On the one hand, a holy person, even if abjectly poor, can be happy and content in the realization that true wealth is found in

God. On the other hand, a greedy, rich person, always aiming for still greater wealth, knows no peace and seeks fulfillment where it cannot be found. Our vow of poverty takes this instinct for wealth, which prompts the human spirit to seek reassurance regarding the future, and destroys it. Our vow quells this instinct and thus rids us of any tainted tendency capable of hiding God from us. Thus, our vow frees us for the one true treasure; that is prayer by which we attain God within ourselves.

Mystical death touches us not only in our goods and property, but also in another of our basic instincts the need to live always. Chastity touches us in the need to prolong life indefinitely. We are not made to die. We know that. There is a repulsion against death because we are destined for immortality. This instinct is deeply rooted within us. We feel this instinct in the essence of our being. It urges human beings to establish a family and to live on in their children, who themselves will beget children.

This instinct gives profound joy to the father and mother of a family who see themselves in the eyes, features, and traits of their children. It engenders the soothing thought that there will always be something of themselves on earth, since they will not entirely die.

The vow of chastity shatters this possibility of a home. And it snatches from our dreams the faces of children who will not be brought to life because we voluntarily renounce this instinct. It removes this assurance that something of ourselves will live forever. This vow entails suffering, just as the vow of poverty, which suppresses the assurance of always having daily bread, entails suffering. In human life there is, then, this instinct to endure that is sundered by the vow of chastity. It strips our heart of its impulses for fatherhood and motherhood. The vow of chastity attacks this instinct by suppressing the possibility of its exercise throughout our life.

Our vows hinder us not only in these instincts that are part of our nature, but also in ways outside of us. They afflict a most lively part of our being in the vow of obedience. It is precisely there that our "self," our "ego," dies. There is nothing greater in human life than liberty, which permits the free disposal of ourselves. God always respects this liberty. Throughout history, we have always ardently exalted our freedom. We are right to do so, for freedom identifies the very nature of the human person.

We really do hold our souls in our hands. Saint Paul tells us that the soul is very fragile, like an earthen vessel, always subject to accidents.[5] That image is true as well as beautiful. The human person acts and is not acted upon. Since we are active and not passive, when we gave our souls to God, we did so freely and willingly. Free will is the most basic and most precious of all human characteristics. Yet, our vow of obedience shatters that freedom. We no longer have that freedom. Therein is a death! In very evocative words, Saint Ignatius Loyola said that, after making his vow of obedience, he had been so slaughtered to the innermost depths of his being that he was "like a corpse."[6] That had to be the case, since a corpse offers no resistance. It can be put here or there at will.

This death is truly total. It involves not only our worldly goods, but also our very selves, of which we have been stripped. Job was stripped of all his possessions and all his servants. However, his own free will had not been "slaughtered."[7] When his friends came to see him, he stood up straight in an attempt to prove that he was not blameworthy. He was defending his free will. As religious, we however no longer control our own lives, since we have consented to a total death.

Thus, what has been realized in Christ by the action of God, our religious profession has made possible in us by our three vows. We have, by this stripping of self, mortally wounded everything in us that is the human "I." We no longer exist. We are being entirely submissive to the will of God. We are literally a new being. This mystical death is thus real, and not merely figurative. Baptism imparts a seed of life in the Christian's soul. That seed can be choked. Likewise, there are religious who mouth the words of this mystical death, but never let its seed grow. They do not let this potency become actualized. Even worse, they live chaotic lives in which this mystical death remains merely a neglected, little plant, kept constantly in darkness and never able to blossom into a living flame of love.

It is essential that this mystical death, once expressed in words, then be expressed in deeds. We die in one stroke by our words and that is easy enough. However, we must then die by our deeds, day-by-day and hour-by-hour. That is much more difficult. To die slowly, gradually and unremittingly until seventy or eighty years old, that is the hardest of all. It is certainly more challenging than to express this death in words amid all the emotion of a grand ceremony. Christ had us in mind, when he spoke of the wise virgins, who had a sufficient supply of the oil of love to keep their lamps ablaze all night long. The foolish virgins, sad to say, had no supply of the oil of love left. In the middle of the night, there was nothing they could do.[8]

Now is the time to consider where we are in relationship to this mystical death. Have we not taken back something of what we at one time gave to God? Have we not, over the humdrum passage of time, taken back something of the world or of ourselves?

The life of prayer is our foremost duty. We are obliged to develop that life to the fullest. It has no limits and thus can grow indefinitely. “The measure of our love of God is to love him without measure.”[9] Let us quell within us whatever remains of our old self. Thus there will remain in us only the eagerness to be like Christ and the Blessed Virgin Mary. Then we, too, will be pure creatures, perfectly pliable in God’s hands. Then, we, too, will be able to find complete happiness in the Infinite Being of God.[10] Amen.

Entrance to Pontoise Monastery Chapel
(on left: shutter for Père Jacques' Guest Room window)

Courtyard in Monastery

Monastery Main Chapel
(photos from the period of the retreat)

Side Chapel where Père Jacques gave his Conferences

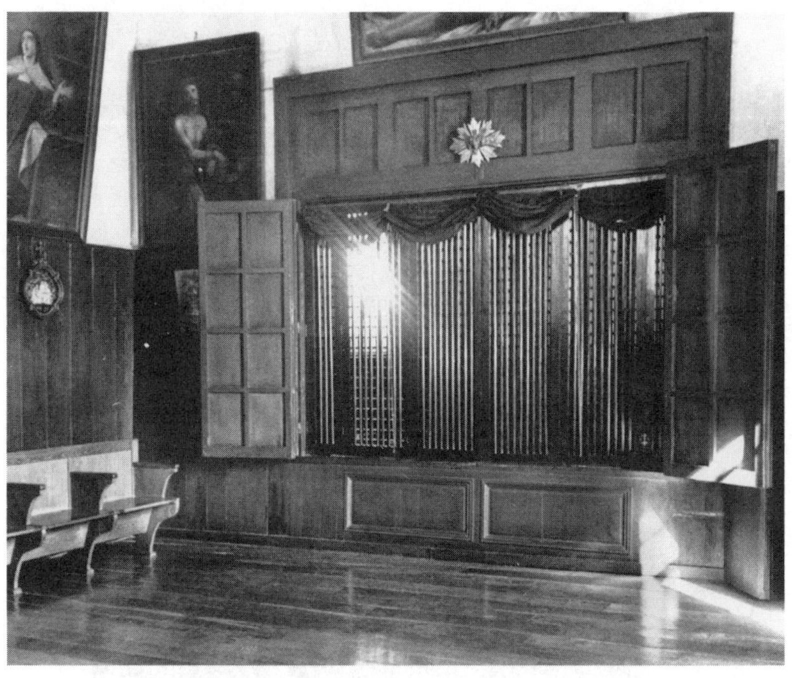

Choir where Nuns heard the Conferences

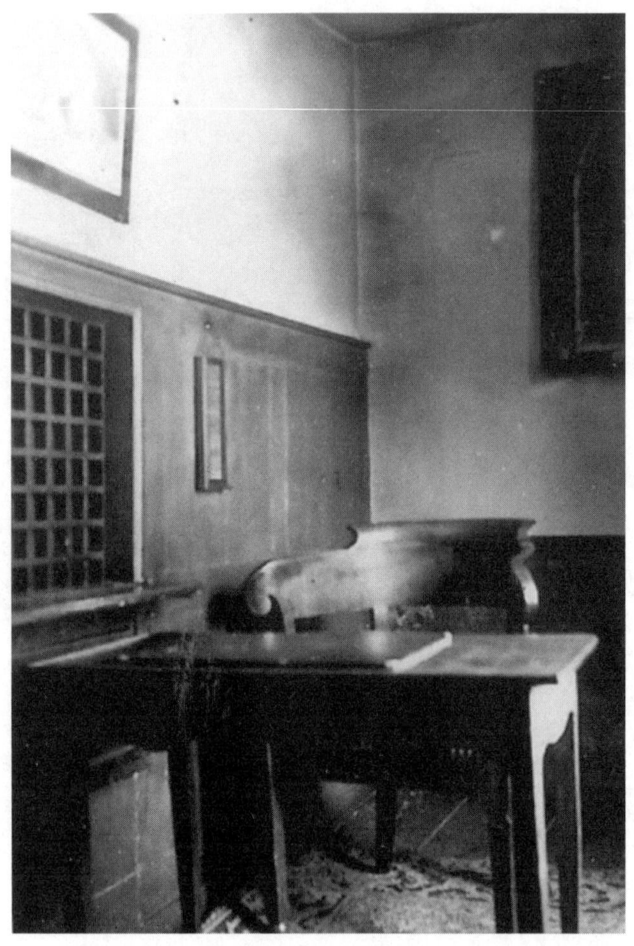

Chair and Grill where Père Jacques gave counseling and the Sacrament of Penance to nuns

Conference 8
Silence
Thursday Evening

When we meditate on the Scriptures and strive to follow Christ closely, we take careful note of what the Gospels tell us about him. We listen to those who knew him and who regularly saw, heard, and served him. From these accounts, we seek to visualize the radiant face of Christ, as it was imprinted on Veronica's veil. When we thus contemplate Christ, we are struck by one of his most characteristic features, his serenity.

Christ is not the type of person whose goal on earth is to enjoy life. Every aspect of Christ's life bears the imprint of his dignified serenity. He is likewise marked by discreet silence. I would like us to meditate together tonight on Christ's silence.

Christ is characteristically serene and silent. In sharp contrast, we see the Apostles as shallow types, bantering among themselves and vying for the foremost places in the kingdom, which they mistakenly conceive in material, rather than spiritual terms. If we examine the conversations of the Apostles, we discover how they posed their questions to Christ and we hear their reactions. Occasionally, their responses are harsh, as when Peter scolded Christ. Far from being quiet, the Apostles are immersed in the noise of the world. Often, at just such moments, Christ quietly comes up behind them. He is silent, because he bears within himself a twofold vision, embracing both heaven and the cross. Even in the human traits of his nature, he habitually portrays a serene silence, because he is already carrying his cross, which cannot be seen. Thus, we should not believe that his Passion began on the night before his death. In truth, the cross that he carried on his shoulders, as he made his way to his crucifixion on Calvary, rested on him from his first day in this world. Yet, he enjoys the beatific vision and his mind is bathed in supernatural light. He possesses all the gifts of the Holy Spirit. Since he knows the Sacred Scriptures through his human intelligence, he can foresee his impending Passion. In palpable, haunting imagery, he discerns the drama of Calvary in all its details. He glimpses the betrayal of his friends and the insults of the crowd, as well as the scourging at the pillar and the crowning with thorns.

The Holy Shroud[1] enables us to discover the full extent of Christ's suffering. Yet, he saw all this ordeal, even the crucifixion itself, in advance. He foresaw his broken bones, his torn flesh and his shattered wrists as elements, not of some distant dream, but of an ever-present vision that accompanied him every day of his life. Likewise accompanying him was an abiding understanding of the human family for whom he is going to lay down his life as proof of his love.

A rarely cited phrase from Saint John's Gospel sheds light on the heart of Christ. That phrase, "He [Jesus] would not trust himself to them…" [Jn 2:24], explains the serene seriousness of his face. Saint John tells us that Christ does not place his trust in his followers, because he knows the secrets in their hearts. Each time he tries to confide in them, the response is a silly lack of understanding. Do you recall the reaction of his closest companions at the time of the Agony in the Garden? They fell asleep!

Are we any different? Do you think that Christ can place his trust in us? Would he say something different if he lived in our midst? Or would it still be: *"Non credebat eis"* ("he would not trust himself to them").

The serene silence of Jesus thus flows from the secret deep within him. Moreover, he likewise enjoys times of deep joy, but they are constantly accompanied by the dreadful image of Calvary and the disappointment derived from human sinfulness. These feelings are always present together. Even at the peak of his Passion, the beatific vision perdures in the depths of his soul. Christ experiences ecstatic moments on Mount Tabor, but even during those moments in the company of Moses and Elijah, he conversed about his Passion for the redemption of sinners.[2]

That serene silence is the hallmark of Christ. He speaks only to impart God's message and only to fulfill his mission by words of consolation, encouragement, and enlightenment. For example, when he was resting at the well in Samaria, he spoke to a local woman. He did not use either empty expressions of politeness or the small talk of the Apostles, who were then dallying in the nearby town. Rather, he said: "If you knew the gift of God..." [Jn 4:10]. Jesus breaks his silence and speaks only to utter words charged with the brilliant light of eternity. He never speaks merely to spread gossip or to satisfy curiosity. Therefore, we are not surprised, as we reflect on this episode, to see Christ absorbed in silence. For God is totally silent. Indeed, the Lord clothes himself in silence.

Perhaps you know of Pascal's cry as he stared at the stars that shone to the limits of the universe. He was seized by the great silence of a winter night aglow with the brightness of the stars and exclaimed: "The eternal silence of the infinite spaces fills me with dread!"[3]

God is eternal silence; God dwells in silence. He is eternal silence because he is the One who has totally realized his own being, because he says all and possesses all. He is infinite happiness and infinite life. All God's works are marked by this characteristic. Contemplate the Incarnation; it was accomplished in the silence of the Virgin Mary's chamber at a time when she was in prolonged silence, her door closed. Our Lord's birth came during the night, while all things were enveloped in silence. That is how the Word of God appeared on earth, and only Mary and Joseph were silently with him. They did not overwhelm him with their questions, for they were accustomed to guarding their innermost thoughts.

The Virgin Mary "kept all these things in her heart, meditating on them in silence" [cf. Lk 2:19]. She had so well absorbed the message of God that even Saint Joseph was unaware of it, and an angel had to come to him in the silence of the night to reveal the great secret [cf. Mt 1:20-21].

The works of God are marked with silence. It is in the silence of prayer and retreat, in the silence of the desert and the forest, that great souls receive their message from God. Recall how Saint Bernard enriched the whole of Europe with silent monasteries. These were stricter still than our type of religious community. Their religious did not have the right to speak or to recreate; they kept total silence. In order to describe the beauty of silence, he used to say: "The oak trees of the forest have been my masters of prayer."[4] Silence is the great master. It speaks to the human heart. Silence is not an empty void; God dwells therein.

Whoever embraces silence, welcomes God and whoever relishes silence, hears God speak. Silence is the echo of God's eternity and the foundation of the rich teaching of Saint John of the Cross. That teaching in all its richness derives from his prison cell at Toledo.[5] During the months of his solitary confinement there, he accepted his isolation and embraced silence. He became imbued with silence. In turn, that silence revealed to him the true value of suffering, which is at the heart of his teaching concerning the ascent to God. Without this treasured silence, John of the Cross would never have become the great mystical Doctor of the Church that he is.

We need to look no further than our own Rule to affirm the necessity of silence in our lives. That Rule seems to say to us: Are you seeking to find God? Then listen to the silence; immerse yourself in silence. Then you will find God by carrying out his will and by fulfilling the austere ideal of Carmel. We must take account of the obligation we have assumed by our vows. We must acknowledge that we are not free to be silent or to be talkative. We entered Carmel and made our religious profession according to the Carmelite Rule precisely to find silence. That is our primary duty. If we do not love silence, then we are hypocritical religious whose lives are a lie. We are, in turn, woeful workers who do not do our job. It would be a contradiction to say seriously that one wishes to be a true Carmelite, yet at the same time rejects silence.

How then are we to regard silence? We can look at silence in two ways: exterior and interior. Material silence, as imposed by the Rule, prohibits all conversation, apart from recreation, except when absolutely necessary. I repeat, except when absolutely necessary! Often, we fabricate pretexts for talking and imagine that, because our chatter flows from these pretexts, we are excused before God. Do you really think that Christ would consider such Sisters to be wise virgins?[6] On the contrary, he would sadly say: "I have no faith in you." A soul that cannot carry the gentle weight of silence and fails to honor the silence of the Rule is lax. Such a Sister demonstrates little inner worth. It is far better to be strict rather than lax in regard to reasons for breaking silence. Those who cannot be drawn to break silence are spiritually sturdy. They embody a wealth of genuine, not pretended, interior prayer. Such is the silence of words. I am, by choice, passing over the question of the regard in which silence is held inside your convent. I know beautifully silent Carmels. I also know one Carmel in decline. That decline began with violations of silence. Soon, everything else there declined. God could not find a dwelling there, for there was no silence.

There is another type of silence, the silence of action. This refinement characterizes the graceful gait and gestures of deeply spiritual persons. They never slam doors; they never noisily push furniture; their movements are never brusque. Such persons can spend the entire day in God's presence. Thus they seem to be accustomed to the eternity of God, who has the time to do everything, yet is never rushed. When religious of this type move about, as they come and go, they always do so slowly and serenely, with discretion and dignity. That is the meaning of exterior silence.

There is, in addition, interior silence. The soul must not be a public square, where there is always a crowd of gossipers or of persons recalled from the past with their tales of suffering and rebuke. Such types, seething at their imagined foes and smarting in their own self-love, are seriously at fault.

There should be nothing like that among us. Silence should penetrate deep within us and occupy every area of our inner home. Thus is our soul transformed into a sanctuary of prayer and recollection.

This evening, let us take to heart this lesson on silence, which brings Christ to us. We can likewise learn this lesson from the ever silent Virgin Mary and all the saints, including our contemporaries, Charles de Foucauld[7] and Saint Thérèse of Lisieux.

Let us ask them for a true love of silence. And what about us? While I was speaking to you this morning, several bombs landed only twenty odd miles from here.[8] Countless victims died. They then had to appear before God and render an account of their lives. We will likewise be called one day to render an account of our lives. If we fail the test, we cannot begin all over again. If our lives have not been marked by silence, charity, and obedience on every level, then we will have been unreliable in our service and unfaithful in our vocation.

I would be remiss, if I did not speak to you, as I have done. I am telling you only what the Lord wants to tell you. Do not think that I am too demanding. It is our ideal that is demanding. I so wish for your Carmel, which I cherish, to be one of the greatest Carmelite convents in France, ablaze with the love of God.

When we meet one day in heaven, we should be filled with joy that we have done everything asked of us. We should have given the Lord, not lip service, but lives of humble, habitual, and complete silence. Such silence allows us to listen to the secret voice of God, like the saints, especially Saint John of the Cross. Such silence allows us to grow in holiness and to become the Lord's guiding lights for the reconstruction of our country. Amen.

Conference 9
Authority
Friday Morning

This morning, let us take up what God in his goodness has given us– this day of silence. As we begin this day, we listen to the silence in which God speaks. We share his secrets as well as his lessons. Let us not disrupt this silence. Instead, let us say only what is strictly necessary. Thus, that living silence, in which God gives himself to us, will remain unbroken. In this silent setting and in the company of the Virgin Mary, let us explore together a problem found even in religious life. Let us examine how Christ dealt with authority.

Our entire life is hierarchically organized. Our religious life, like the Church itself, is based on our concept of authority and our attitude toward authority. Since authority is essential to our community, we must grasp the teaching of both God and the founders of our religious family concerning authority. Only in this way can we live the religious life in its true fullness. We must realize that a religious community is a living, mystical reality and not an accidental assemblage of human beings, eager to share a similar way of life. A religious community embodies continuity and maintains its traditions. It does not belong to those who live there at any given moment. It is more comparable to an entire religious order. Its members neither live nor work for themselves. It is an open-ended, undying undertaking. Its members have a sense of being links in a chain.

Your convent here in Pontoise is one of the cradles of our Order. It remains a model community and one of the first foundations of the Carmelite way of life in France. Its founders came from Spain, the country of our saints. You have marvelous written records and beautifully rich traditions. You are the heirs of your predecessors, not only the most recent ones, but the most ancient as well. From each succeeding generation, all the way back to our foundation, you have received the rich Carmelite traditions and way of life. You must, in turn, transmit this heritage, intact and unaltered, to the generations to follow. That living, beautiful heritage must remain as pure as the day it came to you from the land of Saint Teresa. In viewing your life, your predecessors must be able to recognize the same life that they lived in their day. It is important to realize the seriousness of our commitment. Let us pay particular attention to that commitment, precisely in regard to our life as Carmelites, as envisioned, established and reestablished by Saint Teresa and Saint John of the Cross. That life is solidly based on a hierarchy, derived from authority.

For a fuller understanding of our duty, let us examine Christ's response to the problem of authority. Christ encountered the authority of his parents and of the rulers of the land where he lived. The legally appointed Roman rulers were Herod, the elder, who ruled during his childhood and Herod, the younger, who ruled during his maturity. Most importantly, he encountered the dominant authorities of his home country. Those authorities were the High Priests, Caiaphas and his father-in-law, Annas, along with the Sanhedrin. That body was a type of senate, which governed the country in religious matters. The Sanhedrin actually administered the affairs of the country and shaped opinion, even in regard to private life. The Pharisees were a party that, as an emanation from the Sanhedrin, carried out its thought and directed all aspects of social life.

Within Christ's family, parental authority is very gentle, always thoughtful and delicately expressed. That authority, however, needs to be enlightened, because his parents do not initially realize the full implications of the mission of the child growing up in their home. They are aware of their Son's vocation in broad outline, but its details will become clear to them only as events unfold.

The second type of authority is political and is roundly resented. As a result there are frequent uprisings and insurrections all across the country.

The third type of authority is religious and originates in Jerusalem. This authority is acknowledged as authentic, but it has become corrupted by those responsible for its transmission. The Pharisees gradually stifled the spirit of God's law by virtue of their literal analysis of its every word. They eventually destroyed the very heart of God's law and kept only its skeleton. Thus they turned God into a frighteningly harsh and jealous judge. God is no longer a loving father, but rather a demanding master, held in fear and only rarely sought as a source of love. Now let us examine just how Jesus responded to each of these three types of authority.

First, in regard to his parents, Christ was completely submissive and never evaded their authority. When necessary, he explains to his parents in confidential conversations and gentle words, just who he is and just what lies ahead according to the ancient prophecies. Undoubtedly, on more than one occasion, Jesus had evenings of conversation with Mary, his mother, discussing the meaning of the texts from Isaiah, which describe him as "a man of suffering" [Is 53:3]. It is in this light that we will observe the Virgin Mary along the road Christ followed on his way to Calvary. She is there as a witness, accompanying her son and sharing in his Passion. Yet, she is in no way surprised. He enlightens his parents and clarifies their authority, for they are insufficiently aware of what awaits him in his mission. He does enlighten them, but he remains subject to them. He does point out to them only this: that his calling rests with a higher authority, delegated to them in certain regards. That higher authority is God, his Father.

Although the other authorities are brutally harsh and unjust, Christ subjects himself to them. He never rebelled against the legitimate political authority of his country. When that authority persecutes him and tries to eliminate him, he flees into hiding. However, he does not try to destroy that authority, even though he is almighty. He remains subject to that authority. He responds similarly to the Pharisees, whose power is likewise legitimate. However, when they err doctrinally, he remains respectful, but also proclaims the truth, which he has come to reestablish. In order to reassert the truth, he supports his words with miracles. He says: "I have been sent to preach. If you do not have faith in my words, put faith in my works. I raise the dead to life...Look at my works: are they the works of a man or of God?"[1]

Christ gives the Apostles this advice regarding the Pharisees: "Do what they say, but do not do what they do."[2] Their decrees are legitimate and worthy of respect. Christ drives the merchants out of the temple, because they are degrading that house of prayer. However, he does not drive out either the high priest or his assistants. Christ takes action against the abuse, but he leaves the authority in place. When he is brought before the High Priest, he simply says: "If I have spoken wrongly, testify to the wrong; but if I have spoken rightly, why do you strike me?" [Jn 18:23].

Before Caiaphas,[3] he is content simply to assert his divine mission and then state: "You would have no power over me, if it had not been given to you from above" [Jn 19:11].

In matters concerning Roman rule, he declares: "Then repay to Caesar what belongs to Caesar and to God what belongs to God" [Mt 22:21]. Thus we see that Christ was always subject to authority of every sort. Many years later, Saint Paul, imbued with this teaching, will instruct the new Christians in Rome and its territories: "Obey the Emperor and his social authority. You must obey legitimate authority in all matters that do not violate your conscience."[4]

We discover the inner secret of Christ's attitude in this statement: "You would have no power over me, if it had not been given to you from above" [Jn 19:11]. No human person whosoever has the right to give an order to another human person on any merely human basis. Let us suppose, for sake of discussion, that there exist only human beings and that a human person, as such, has no right to give an order to another human person. Now, conversely, let us suppose that no human person has the right to degrade himself by obeying another human person as such. However, the human person is inherently social and not an isolated individual. The human person does not exist alone as an individual, but rather exists in a unique social context. The human person is the foundation stone of the social unit we call the family.

Human beings are social beings. There can be no society without a head, without a hierarchy, without someone responsible, without someone in command. At the head of every little social cell, there are responsible persons who have the right to command and who exact the duty of obedience. It is not in their own name that they command. They command because they represent the creator, the sovereign Master, the One who has appointed them head of the household or the sacred cell or the assembly of the people who live in the social group of which they are the head. God alone has the right to command, because God is the creator. God delegates his divine authority to those persons who are hierarchically appointed to exercise power over others. Christ submitted himself to authorities whom he infinitely surpassed and who often had fallen from honor or were morally stained. In so doing, he gave us a great lesson: it was God his Father whom he was obeying.

Indeed, it is remarkable that authority can sometimes reside in human beings who are personally unworthy. In the same way the splendor of the priesthood can sometimes be bestowed on hands that basely besmirch and singularly sully that priesthood. There are unworthy priests. However, when their hands bless or their lips pronounce the words of consecration, it is the marvelously beautiful God who acts; it is Jesus who is present in the host and pardons the sinner. The priest, sometimes unworthy as an individual, does not negate his priesthood and does not defile God who acts through him. It is always God who acts, God who speaks, and God who must be respected. As you can see, it is necessary to have a very clear appreciation of the source of legitimate authority. It is God who is there and who speaks. It is God whom one disobeys by scorning authority. In short, there is a divorce between God and ourselves when we disregard legitimate authority.

We can be sure of this. In each of our monasteries, regardless of the particular superior, there is a legitimate authority, which we do not have to discuss or examine. That authority is legitimately constituted; in fact, it is God himself there present. We can likewise be sure, since we are human persons with our own temperaments, that there may well be differences of opinion and all sorts of little irritations in daily life. These human "foibles," as they were called by a wise, old priest, should not hinder us. Recall the expression: put two saints together and they will make themselves suffer. There may well be difficulties, but that is not important. What is important is God and his voice in all its fullness. Therefore, in response to the commands of legitimate authority, we should reply with a total gift of ourselves. Our human nature must not quibble or deceive. Our response must be complete–a legitimate subject to a legitimate superior without comment, excuse, or reservation.

A superior issues an honest clear and correct order, because it is God who speaks and God alone who should speak. In turn, the response should be equally and fully honest, even if there seems to be an error of some sort on the part of the superior. In such a situation, the subject should point out the perceived error and be at peace. The response should be complete and devoid of duplicity, which produces only half-hearted obedience and is satisfied by a less than total clash with God. There must be harmony among those given over to God. We may be able to deceive a superior, but we cannot deceive God. He is omniscient and well aware of any ill will, even in the quiet of our cell, and of any incomplete commitment, even in the corner of the choir.

We must not be like that. The spiritual life must be a life of light and virtue. God can come to us only if we are totally and transparently open to him and give ourselves unreservedly to him.

The answer to the great problem of authority is God alone. Therefore, let us see God alone, as we spiritedly stamp out whatever within us that is not totally submissive to God. Then, God will find in us a completely receptive dwelling place. If you find yourself complaining that your prayer is lifeless and filled with distraction, then empty your inner dwelling of yourself! We should be completely submissive subjects. We should welcome even disagreeable, demanding orders. Thus we will be responding to God, as he wishes. Thus we will attain a truly exalted life. Amen.

Conference 10
The Cross: To Baptize Suffering and Happiness
Friday Evening

The profound problem of evil is a scandal that keeps many people far from God and drives many others away from him. Is it moral evil and sin at work? Yes, but there is more at work. Is it moral evil among those who should be setting an example? Again, yes, but even more so, it is physical evil and suffering. This is evil that we all witness. Take war, for example, with its deliberate destruction of cities and its unjustifiable slaughter of the elderly and the innocent, of women and children. Such is the scourge of war. Then there are diseases and calamities of all types: earthquakes, floods, droughts and monsoons which produce massive, multifaceted suffering. Children are torn away from their parents and families are broken up.[1]

How often I have heard my friends express their thoughts on this problem! They ask: "Do you think that, if God existed and were omnipotent, he would allow such slaughter? Would he tolerate the triumph of evil and let thieves live in peace? Would he permit deceivers to get the better of decent people? Would he let human passions be the strongest force on earth?" The problem of evil, as we can surely see, is the most profound of problems. Understandably, therefore, Christ wanted to resolve this problem. Accordingly, he willed to live here on earth for several years and then, engulfed in suffering, to die in public.

As we have already noted, the Word made flesh could have gained God's forgiveness of all possible sin by simply coming into our world. This simultaneously spontaneous, yet divine humiliation was so meritorious that all possible sin could have been wiped away by a simple request by the Word made flesh to his Father. Christ did not will to do so. Instead, he died under circumstances as wretched as those of the most afflicted on earth.

Christ's body was both extremely sensitive and perfectly balanced. Likewise, bear in mind Christ had an especially tender soul, which keenly experienced whatever happened in his body. A person who has been poorly raised, never treated with consideration and deprived of the refinements of education, feels physical ordeals and privations far less acutely than a highly educated, polished person.

Christ's perfect sensitivity produced unexpected results. His Passion, the sum of all his physical, emotional, and spiritual suffering, was completely crushing. We need only to look at him in the Garden of Olives, or when he is stripped of his garments or as he drags himself to Calvary. His only wish is to conform fully to God's will.

At the first moment of his Passion, blood gushed out like sweat on his body, as a result of the revulsion he experienced in the face of what awaited him. Such was his profound reaction to the pain he experienced. Thus, we see that, with full awareness, he freely willed to undergo this overwhelming ordeal of suffering in public. In truth, he had lived this Passion from the start of his life on earth.

God created us not for suffering but for happiness, above all and without exception. He wills our happiness in order that we may enjoy with him the fullness of joy. The misfortune is that we human beings do not know how to be happy. We learn everything about happiness except what is essential.

What must we do to be happy? We seek all roads to happiness, yet do not find it. We spend time seeking it. It is a daily preoccupation. People even change jobs in their pursuit of that goal. We ourselves have no other instinct than to be happy. And we are right; all our being aspires to happiness. We have been so created by God. We desire to be happy like God.

God knows no alteration to his infinite happiness. Happiness is positive; evil is negative. God cannot make something negative. Evil does not come from God, because it is an absence of being, a lack of perfection. Happiness is the fullness of being, the overflowing of being. Evil is definitely not a divine work.

Since Adam and Eve, people have been seeking happiness. Like Adam and Eve, they have sought their happiness by doing evil. We do the same thing. We begin the cycle again! All who preceded us and did not find happiness were deceived. In vain they heard theses words: "That's not the way to happiness." They did not listen. They wanted to discover their own roads to happiness. Those roads proved to be dead ends. They had to turn around and take another direction. What a waste of time!

If we only listened to Christ who came to teach the world true happiness! Against true human happiness, there is, or appears to be, a great obstacle: the evil of suffering.

There are two ways of dealing with suffering. The first way is to eliminate its causes by taking every precaution against it. When it does come, we try to whisk it away or suppress it by all the means at our disposal. However, there is a second way to deal with suffering: we can "baptize" it.

In general, most people adopt the first way. There is not a single human being who does not experience suffering in one form or another. Sooner or later, even those who now seem to go through life singing, with the assurance of health and strength, are going to have their share of bitterness, grief, and sadness. To be sure, most people want to destroy misery. They want to eliminate it by avoiding it, strangling it, brushing it aside, or dismissing it. They do not want to tolerate it. Almost all parents are eager to remove suffering from their children's path. They are anxious to lessen and suppress such suffering when it strikes.

Christ knew that this way of dealing with suffering is simply a kind of stopgap measure, and does not strike the root of the evil. It can work for only a few hours or days or months. Christ adopted another way–a deeply divine, definite way. Christ converted suffering into happiness. Suffering can still come, but it is no longer a sadness. Christ has taught us to overtake suffering at its source. There, where it springs up, we can seize and transform it; there, we can change its nature and make it a source of happiness. Since Christ chose suffering for himself, suffering is not a curse or a plague to be avoided at any price. Christ welcomed the cross and even said, "He who wishes to come after me must take up his cross every day and follow in my footsteps" [Lk 9:23].

We have already considered God's preparation of Mary to be the mother of his eternal Son. What extraordinary supernatural gifts God poured out on her at the moment of her creation and throughout her life. Would God not have loved his mother to have given her such exceptional gifts? But he also gave her the fullest measure of suffering. Do we not call the Virgin Mary, "Our Lady of the Seven Sorrows?"[2] Since the number seven is considered a sign of perfection, it follows that her suffering represented the epitome of living, human suffering. That is the destiny of Christ's mother. It makes us stop and think. We can understand how Christ would be willing to carry such a weight of sorrow, but why would he have so weighed down his mother? Would anyone of us be willing to heap such a weight of suffering on our mother? We would gladly be killed, if necessary, to spare our mother pain or suffering. What kind of criminal would not weep at the shame inflicted on his mother by his sentence?

At no moment did Christ conceal any element of his Passion from his mother. There has to be an unfathomable mystery in this freely willed suffering for God to treat his mother in that way. Christ treated all the saints, without exception, in the same way. To the measure that he loved a soul, to that degree he saddled it with trials.

What else would you expect? Christ is not someplace other than on the cross, with his head torn open by the crown of thorns and his body pierced by the whips and nails of his executioners. Yes, Christ is on the cross. Christ without the cross would be too bland; the cross without Christ would be too severe. If you truly wish to do nothing apart from Christ, then you must meet him and embrace him, where he is.

You are familiar, are you not, with the vision of Saint Francis, depicted in a remarkable painting.[3] Saint Francis is portrayed embracing Christ on the cross. But Our Lord draws his own right arm from the cross in order to embrace his friend Francis. When Christ embraces someone, that person's head is touched by the Crown of Thorns on the Lord's head and the mark of the cross is left on him. When Christ grasps someone's hand, the mark of blood is left on him, because the Lord's mangled hand is covered with blood. To espouse Christ is to espouse the cross. To be his companions, we must faithfully follow him, as he carries the cross and as he hangs on the cross.

Christ who came to teach us to be happy found an abundance of suffering that upset human happiness. He has transformed that suffering by teaching us that there is a force, a lever, to raise the world. It is redemption! When we have said that, suffering is no longer suffering nor something evil. Through his suffering, Christ has redeemed the world. Through her suffering, the Virgin Mary has shared in the redemptive work of her son. Each of us through our suffering can personally participate in the work of redemption as well. What an honor! With what tender affection God treats us! He could redeem us without our efforts, but he did not wish it so.

Instead, God grants us the richly comforting and inspiring sense that we participate in our own redemption. The undeserved solace thus gained can be transformed by our own self-imposed suffering or by our acceptance of providentially sent trials. Thus we can regain our dignity and innocence, while experiencing the inner joy of being collaborators in the attainment of our own true happiness. Each one of us, through our suffering in union with Christ, can share in the redemption of our families and friends, our enemies and people all over the world. Our only limit is our generosity. If only the whole world knew that! If people had only tasted the bitter fruit of redemptive suffering and had only understood the great human dignity attained by experiencing this bitter happiness, then there would be no scandal in suffering. Then suffering would no longer spark revolt, but would be a source only of happiness. Suffering, when seen as a constituent part of redemption, becomes for us something splendid and well worth the pain of living it out.

You know how conscientious our spiritual mother, Saint Teresa, always was. I leave you with these reflections on her life. She so thoroughly understood the concept of the baptism and transfiguration of suffering by Christ that she was concerned if by sunset she had not experienced any trials in the course of the day. She had adopted as her motto, *"aut mori aut pati."*[4] She would say at such times: "Are you going to forget me?" "Are you going to stop loving me?" *"Aut mori aut pati."*

Saint Teresa was well aware that God afflicts those whom he loves when she said: "Oh, to die and thus to see you! But, if you will for me to live longer here on earth, then please grant me suffering, so that I will not waste the time."[5] Life without suffering is a waste of time. Every hour not united to God's will is an hour squandered. Trials can take many forms, such as strict silence, distasteful duties, exhausting work and very trying acts of obedience. Yet, every trial we evade represents time lost.

I call on you, my God, and on you, ever Virgin Mary, for you have never wasted your time. I call on you, John of the Cross, Teresa of Avila, and Thérèse of the Child Jesus for you have never wasted the time given to you for your own sanctification and for God's work of redemption. Teach me to love. Teach me how to implement the beautiful motto, *"Aut mori, aut pati."* Oh, to die, my God! But if you will that I still live, then grant me suffering, which becomes the source of happiness, as suffering baptized. Amen.

Conference 11
Hope and Abandonment
Saturday Morning

The study of Christ is an open-ended undertaking. It would take several years to make a thorough study of the inner life of Christ, as well as the precise exercise of all his natural and supernatural faculties. We do not have to do that during this retreat. We have a simpler aim: to discern the essential characteristics of Christ and to see how he conducted himself in situations such as we ourselves experience in our daily life.

When we consider the three theological virtues, which should be the foundation of our spiritual life, we note that Christ did not need faith. In certain liturgical celebrations, we chant these words, which are applicable to Christ: now there are three virtues, faith, hope and love, but only love endures forever.[1] In heaven there is only one theological virtue and that is love. Love will endure forever, whereas the other two theological virtues are intended to grant us access to God during our life on earth. Christ did not need faith, for he experienced the beatific vision. In the lofty language of Saint Paul, we can believe only what we cannot see. Christ's love infinitely exceeds ours. Did Christ possess the virtue of hope? Did he possess that virtue portrayed so enthusiastically by Péguy in his splendidly moving pages on the Divine Person? Péguy presents God as speaking and saying repeatedly: What amazes me is that people still have hope. They are obliged to have faith, with all its beauty. However, the fact that they still have hope, despite daily disappointments, despite suffering when they expected joy and despite sickness when they wanted good health, amazes me. The fact that people sing their songs of hope at the start of each new day, absolutely amazes me![2]

Did Christ possess the virtue of hope? As formally defined in the Act of Hope, the answer is no. Christ did not hope for grace in this life and glory in the life to come, since he already possessed both. However, he did possess a certain type of hope–his surrender to God's providential plan. The totality of his human nature, his body and soul, his mind and will, his tenderness, and emotions, surrenders to God with tranquil trust. In his immediate vision, Christ contemplates God in his immense power, his infinite wisdom and his limitless love, This discovery stirs up in his heart a total, confident surrender to God. Thus, Christ places his complete self in the hands of God, whom he knows is his Father.

Only rarely do we meet someone who admits offenses against hope. The priest in confession often encounters doubts against faith, lapses of charity, theft, impurity, spite, anger, gluttony, and all the other sins. However, he rarely encounters offenses against hope, in general, and against surrender to Divine Providence, in particular. Nonetheless, such sins are possibly the most painful to God, because they strike at his heart.

Please, excuse me for using human language in speaking of God. Yet, we must make such use of our language, despite its limitations, in reference to God. God is the fullness of love, as Christ said over and over again. We ourselves say the "Good God."[3]

Yes, God is good and lack of trust in God is a direct denial of his goodness. It is like saying to God: "You have no heart!" Here on earth, when we say: "You have no heart," the other person is deeply hurt, precisely because one of the loftiest human qualities is to "have heart," which makes us good.

The human person is presumably good. If that is not the case, we call the person a beast or a brute. The more fully a person approximates the highest level of human development, the more expansive is the reach of that person's charity. In this sense, the saints and preeminently the Blessed Virgin Mary were singularly good. We spontaneously appeal to the saints because they are good. We can be sure that they will never rebuff us and will always help us. People flock to Saint Thérèse, the Little Flower, because they know how true are her words: "I will spend my heaven doing good on earth."[4]

To paraphrase Saint Thomas,[5] saints are those who have taken on the ways of God. They have been transformed into God's image by allowing God so to fashion them. A saint is a person who is full of love. When we sin against hope, we effectively say to God: "I reject you. You are wicked and heartless. I have no confidence whatsoever in your goodness." Such a sin, while perhaps less visibly flagrant than certain sins against chastity, is still grievous, because it occurs in a realm of only minimal mitigating circumstances. Such a sin assumes its gravity from its direct reference to God. Most sins derive from human weakness; however, sins against hope strike directly against God's goodness and wisdom. Where does a person who sins against hope stand in relationship to God's love?

Precisely because she is one of the greatest saints who ever lived, Saint Thérèse of Lisieux clearly understood the meaning of surrender to God and its accompanying attitude of complete spiritual trust. She used to use this somewhat innocent, but very expressive metaphor: "I am a toy in God's hands, a little ball for the Child Jesus to play with."[6] There was, however, another voice that was her cruelest trial and haunted her heart, even during her prayers and her thanksgiving after Communion. This sneering, sarcastic voice never ceased saying to her: "You are mistaken; heaven does not exist; God is an illusion; you are wasting your life. Listen to that piano; there is a lively, joyful party over there, which you will really enjoy. You have foolishly given up everything. There you are, with all your silence, all your poverty, all your fasting, and all your chills, all completely useless!" That voice haunted her not for a few hours, not for a month, but unceasingly, as her body grew ever weaker. Even when she was at the brink of death, with her vitality ebbing away, this humble little Carmelite echoed the words of Job: "Slay me though he [God] might, I will wait for him" [Job 13:15]. Such a saint knows the real meaning of hope and the requirements of true trust in God, when she says: "Good God, our Father, thy will be done." At that moment, she is expressing her trust, not her dreams.

Others merely dream and do not follow through on their words. They are content to fantasize about surrendering their lives to God; during periods of prayer and silence, they envision great future projects. However, they are incapable of fulfilling the actual demands of their daily lives. They are in a constant state of waiting, as they nourish their fantasies, without ever implementing them. Thus they waste both their time and their lives.

There is a certain state of hope found in Christ and likewise found in Saint John of the Cross. Such was his state of hope, when he was in his prison cell, tormented by his own brother friars, who should have been charitable, but were not. Such was his state of surrender to God, when he was bowed down by hunger and scourged until be bled. Such was his state of hope, when he was locked up for months in his narrow cell, with neither light nor air and with no way even to stand up. We often speak of surrender to God. In all honesty, we should neither utter nor hear that expression without a swell of joy in our hearts and an air of peace in our souls. I hope that all of you have not merely read but have digested, sentence by sentence, the splendid little book by Father de Caussade, entitled: *Abandonment to Divine Providence*. This work, along with its superb accompanying *Letters*, is remarkable for its simplicity, devoid of theological jargon, yet filled with spiritual nourishment throughout its hundred pages.[7]

On what doctrinal foundations does this state of abandonment rest? On our part, this state of abandonment is our finest possible gift to God, as well as the filial relationship we should maintain with God. Its doctrinal foundation is drawn from what we know about God as infinite Wisdom. What beautiful implications there are to the words *Sapientia* and *Sapere*![8] Likewise, we must consider the Omnipotence and Love of God. However, since God is utterly simple, Wisdom, Omnipotence, and Love are inseparably united in the divine nature. These three divine attributes Wisdom, Omnipotence, and Love, are manifestations of the eternal activity and immutable actuality of God, who is Love.

The words of our mother Saint Teresa show us that she knew precisely how to communicate the fundamental doctrine of the state of abandonment. "God is all powerful and he loves me,"[9] she used to say. All is said when that is said! Consequently, all that comes from God is wise and loving. We have only to accept his will with thanksgiving and adoration; it is what is best for us. The love he gives us is a gift from the best of fathers to the child whom he loves; it is supernatural wealth poured out on his child who cries out to his father.

Since God is all-powerful, his will embraces everything that happens in the world and in our lives. His will embraces everything that touches or occupies us, whether it is a threat or a task or an event. His will embraces the grace of prayer, a conversation with our Superior, an accident, a sorrow, a friendship, an antipathy, even our cowardice, our fears, and our sins. Whatever enriches or diminishes our being absolutely everything, even the least particle is willed and ordained by God either directly or indirectly. God permits our faults indirectly. He lets them be, for they have a place in his plan. Even those enormous faults of ambition and pride that upset the whole world have their place in God's plan. God created beauty and we spend our time defiling his work. God follows us and unwearyingly repairs what our hands have foolishly degraded despite its original magnificence. Each second we live prolongs our existence. Each succeeding second is offered to us as a gift from the hand of God, our omnipotent creator. When we have understood this truth and when we live continuously each day in a real state of authentic abandonment, we have at our disposal a new way of ceaselessly communing with God.

There are two ways of communing with God. The first is the sacramental way, by reception of the sacred host, which allows us to bear Christ's presence within ourselves. The second and unceasing way consists of God giving himself to us every moment of every day of our lives. In this way, God comes to us in the form of a duty, a joy or a sorrow. God comes to us in other persons, such as an unappealing sister with whom we have to work or a congenial sister with whom we sit at recreation. In all these situations, it is God who comes to us, but we do not realize his presence. Yet, whatever the form behind which he hides and whatever the garb in which he presents himself, he is the God of Wisdom, Omnipotence, and Love without limits.

We will be saints, with holiness like that of the Blessed Virgin Mary, Saint John of the Cross, Saint Teresa of Avila and the

Little Flower, when God comes to us no longer in divine radiance, but in the form of a crushing threat to our life. Such was the experience of Christ in his Passion. Even if our human nature recoils in fear and trembling, we will be able to commune with God within the recesses of our soul through abandonment. There lies the key to God's love and peace.

I would like now to speak to you about the ongoing action by which God presents himself to those generous souls committed to him. God makes use even of our faults, by letting them serve to break certain tendencies to pride. Some faults are favors from God, because they make us blush and lower our heads toward the ground. God allows these faults and does not prevent them, because we are so pig-headed that, only by being thrown down on the ground and rolling around in the slime, do we come to realize that we ourselves are slime and there is no other way for us to break out of our pride. There is nothing more insufferable than a person, especially a religious, who claims to be very virtuous and takes all the credit, forgetting that "everything comes from above."[10] All our gifts come from God, not from ourselves. In his goodness and by his insistent action, God unceasingly pursues us and shows us our own worthlessness. Thus, God reduces us to an awareness of our own fallen state and our actual inability to do anything whatsoever of and by ourselves.

Sincere souls, who are actually making spiritual progress, tend to have a sense that they are regressing, despite their generous efforts. That reaction is mistaken, as an alert spiritual director can reassuringly point out. Nonetheless, such a soul remains sadly troubled by an unyielding sense of unworthiness. It must pass through that trial. The saints passed through similar trials. They wept and beat their breasts, calling themselves the world's worst sinners. And, they were right! What they saw in themselves made them react as they did, because God showed them their inner selves in his light.

In conclusion, we do not have to decide whether to embrace or reject this state of abandonment. As religious, you have freely come to Carmel. Just as a man is free to marry or to become a priest, so a person is free to enter, when so called, into religious life or to remain in the world. God does not require a person to respond to his call under pain of sin. Now, however, we have already made our choice. We have committed ourselves by our vows. Having made our choice, we must now strive for perfect fulfillment of our Rule.

God is our master, who watches over us, his workers. Just as the blacksmith must tend to his forge, so we must tend to our task. We will be either good or bad workers in God's eye and will be compensated accordingly. Of those who should have been the salt of the earth, but were not, our Lord says: "It is no longer good for anything but to be thrown out..." [Mt 5:13]. We do not have a choice to live or not to live a life of abandonment to Divine Providence. Such a life is our occupation and we must fulfill its requirements. We must be devoted children, who place our trust in our Father and do not foolishly spurn him. Whatever we do, we do to God!

We must aim to live with confidence in God. Through abandonment to Divine Providence, we live a life of hope, which refreshes our souls and unites us with God at every moment until this spiritual communion becomes our eternal state.

Finally, I want to leave with you this profound prayer, to be recited time and again: "O God, I wish to be fully what I am." There is no prayer more beautiful, more pleasing or more powerful in God's eye than this simple prayer. It is the *fiat* of the Father. In a special way, it supplements the "Our Father," which Christ taught. "O God, I wish to be just what I am for as long as you so will; I am aware of an evil strain deep within me. That strain spawns egotism, infidelity and hostility, leading to moodiness, laziness, and self-indulgence. I wish to be fully what I am. For, I know that you are all powerful and could change me in an instant. Yet, at the same time, you are infinitely loving and offer me whatever is for my best.I have total trust in you.You are all powerful and you love me!" [11] Amen.

Conference 12
The Holy Spirit, Master of Prayer
Saturday Evening

At the outset of this retreat, I noted that we do not have to choose our way of life. Since we are contemplative religious, we must be persons of prayer. That prayer should pervade our daily life. Our hours lived out in monastic solitude should constitute a state of prayer. Such prayer centers on the quest of God, whom we must come to know in and through Christ. However, in order to know how to pray properly and how to progress each day on the path of prayer, we need a master of prayer. Christ himself specifies who is the teacher provided for this difficult, but necessary instruction. Our master of prayer is the Holy Spirit.

This evening, I would like to speak with you about the Holy Spirit, described in the title of a book from the turn of the century as *The Forgotten Paraclete*.[1] How many baptized Christians never even think of the Holy Spirit and live as if he really did not exist? They could readily repeat the response of the faithful at Antioch, who, when asked if they had received the Holy Spirit, replied: "We have never even heard that there is a Holy Spirit" [Acts 19:3].

As for the rest of us, is the Holy Spirit really our master of prayer? To be sure, twice a day, we begin our common prayer with an invocation of the Holy Spirit. Most likely, in the quiet of our rooms, we occasionally call upon the Holy Spirit before beginning a task. But in all honesty, how many of us consciously consider the orientation of our invocation of the Holy Spirit, when we begin our prayer and, there at our place in chapel, ask to learn how to pray? We say, "Come, Holy Spirit," but our heart is not involved, as we mouth the words. How can we really wish for the Holy Spirit to come to teach us to pray, when we routinely utter words devoid of spiritual urgency and heartfelt longing?

The Holy Spirit is the master of prayer. It is not surprising that God has given us this master to teach us the difficult lessons of prayer, since prayer is a supernatural work of love. There is no prayer that is not a work of love. Recall how Saint Teresa of Avila defined prayer as "an exchange of friendship with God."[2]

Among the difficult types of prayer can be listed the prayer of "simple regard." In the life of the Curé of Ars we find a magnificent example of this type of simple, profound, intense prayer that can scale the highest spiritual summits. Infused mystical prayer, which must be our prayer, is just that: a simple look, an exchange of looks. Each evening as night was falling, the Curé of Ars[3] saw a field laborer enter his country church. He remained there a long time, his lips not moving.

After observing him a while, the intrigued Curé asked him, "What do you do here?" "Why I pray to Jesus." "And what do you say to him in your prayer?" "I say nothing to him; I look at him and he looks at me!" This man had received no instruction from any human master. He had read no theological treatise; he was ignorant of the ways of prayer. However, he had been instructed by the Holy Spirit, and the Spirit had revealed to him this method of prayer. He knew that the best prayer was a simple exchange of "looks" between God and the soul. Such a look said everything because it came from the heart, and the heart does not need words. The heart communicates with a single glance.

You have undoubtedly experienced in your own life a deep, legitimate affection for your father or mother, sister or brother, when nothing is said. At that moment a simple look or handshake says it all; the entire heart is moved. The best in oneself goes out to meet the best in another, who experiences this deep affection. Those moments and those very simple expressions of love between God and ourselves are the essence of prayer.

When we gaze upon God, we experience God gazing upon us. When we smile at God, God smiles at us. There is an exchange between God's tender heart and ours. There is a dynamic, powerful communication, based not on words, but on actual experience; there is an embrace of love. Every expression of supernatural love has always been attributed to the Holy Spirit. Within the Trinity, the Holy Spirit is the living, limitless prayer of God, the love that unites the Father and the Son. Try as we may to discover the Spirit, we perceive only his faint rays. Even his name itself outstrips our imagination. The names Father and Son relate to the process of human generation here on earth, but not so the Holy Spirit!

In many respects, the word Spirit is unfortunate. We should use the term "breath," corresponding to the Greek word *"pneuma."* Thus the Spirit is the "breath" that unfailingly unites the Father and the Son. Within the Trinity, all works of love are attributed to the Spirit, as well as all actions, described in human language as "exterior to God." Here again, the terminology we use is unfortunate. In truth, there is nothing "exterior to God." However, we must rely on human language, despite its limitations. Accordingly, in all works "exterior to God," whatever reflects divine love is attributed to the Holy Spirit. At the creation of the world the Spirit of God hovered over the waters. There the seeds of life were sown and life is a work of love. Thus, it was the Holy Spirit who hovered mysteriously over the chaos in order to bring about life.

The Incarnation is likewise a work of love. The Holy Spirit knew the Virgin Mary in advance, for he taught her the rich lessons of prayer. Consider Mary's long hours immersed in prayer concerning her community and the drama of divine love for all humanity; concerning the fall of the human race and the mighty power of God. In those silent hours of prayer, the Holy Spirit inflamed Mary's heart and swept her up into the bosom of the triune God. There, Mary was immersed in the ocean of God's being. Mary's hours of prayer! Therein, God's presence attains a new and unprecedented level. God is going to ask Mary to allow her body to bring about his Incarnation. He is going to embody himself in a mysterious way in the offspring to be born of her pure blood, divinely preserved from every stain of sin. The Holy Spirit is the author of this wondrous work of love. "The Holy Spirit will come upon you, and the power of the Most High will overshadow you. Therefore, the child to be born will be called holy, the Son of God" [Lk 1:35].

Throughout the whole world, the Holy Spirit carries out the work of sanctifying every baptized person. The Holy Spirit dwells in every baptized soul, infusing divine life and bestowing the first lesson in prayer. On the very day of baptism, the initial instruction in prayer is imparted by the Holy Spirit to the soul, that then enters into living, personal contact with God. Sad to say, the vast majority of the baptized remain at this initial level. Far more rare are those who pursue their spiritual schooling in full awareness that they have available to them a teacher eager to impart his priceless lessons on prayer. Likewise, as religious, we invoked the Holy Spirit on the day of our solemn profession, which renewed and intensified the spiritual project begun at our baptism. We sang the hymn, "Come, Holy Ghost, Creator Blessed," which imparts an entirely new meaning to the day of profession or the receiving of the habit. At such moments of profound spiritual renewal, we focus on creating a new person. The old self has just disappeared in death. We implore the Holy Spirit to come and create a beautifully new being, enlightened by his wisdom and teaching.

How urgent it is for us to call on the Holy Spirit, as we enroll, figuratively speaking, in the University of Divine Love. A monastery is that type of school. There, the incomparable master of prayer, the Holy Spirit, teaches the most advanced and most rewarding courses on the love of God.

What do we have to do in order to benefit fully from our master's lessons? First, we must consciously acknowledge the impossibility of progressing in prayer apart from our master. Recall the words of Jesus to his apostles: "It is better for you, if I go away. For, if I do not go away, I cannot send you the Holy Spirit. But, when I am at my Father's side, I will send the Holy Spirit to you, and he will teach you everything I have told you."[4] Therein lies the role of the Holy Spirit, who now comes into our souls to reveal what Christ had once said, without being understood. The Spirit illuminates that teaching, step by step, with his interior light. He endows the soul with three extraordinary gifts, uniquely pertinent to prayer. These gifts are intelligence, knowledge, and wisdom. We can see among these three gifts a hierarchy that spiritual writers have pointed out in reference to our relationship with God.

First, there is philosophical knowledge, attained by a process of reasoning. Such knowledge is totally and coldly deductive, as in the solution to a problem. Then there is theological knowledge, attained by applying the laws proper to revealed doctrine, the full force of reason and the careful scrutiny of language. Thus, new and previously hidden truth emerges. While this approach is more rewarding than the first process, it can still be completely human.

There remains a third type of knowledge, an experimental knowledge of God. This is a knowledge of the heart, attained by meeting God, by sharing his embrace, by remaining together and walking side by side with him. Providing that we never turn aside, there is a continuous exchange of glances between God and us. All day long, he nourishes us with his tender love, pouring out of his heart. This type of knowledge is totally different from the other two. Only this type of knowledge can satisfy the human heart. The Holy Spirit tends to give this gift to very humble souls as well as to very learned theologians, who despite their prestige, are often far less wise than the very humble souls who know God by experience. This last type of knowledge can be attained only through the gift of wisdom, conferred by the Holy Spirit.

These gifts are like supernatural powers, grafted onto the soul. They enable the soul to soar up, to meet and to savor God. The Latin root of the word wisdom is *"sapere,"* meaning to taste and to digest. Accordingly, when we know God through wisdom, we are nourished by God and relish the pure joy of being absorbed in God.

What sublime knowledge! However, in order for the Holy Spirit to work within us, we must first acknowledge his existence and his presence within us. Only rarely do we find books written about this great mystery. One such study is an excellent, but hard to find, doctoral dissertation, entitled: *The Indwelling of the Holy Spirit in the Souls of the Just.*[5] What a wonderful work! Think about this: we can go anywhere at all and can still hear the Holy Spirit speak to us, provided we remain silent. The Spirit speaks only to souls absorbed in silence. If we are not silent, we drive away the Spirit, rejecting his presence and quelling his voice. When everyone is speaking to us, the Holy Spirit stills his voice and stops his lessons. However, if we are silently attentive, we hear him all day long.

These gifts stir up movements of grace, such as an inner suggestion or a generous impulse to accept something disagreeable, like a nasty comment. Such subtle, sensitive inner promptings are lessons of the Holy Spirit. They are also lessons in prayer, because the more our souls are sensitized to the touch of the Holy Spirit, the more we throb with the breath of his love and the more we become gently permeated with prayer. If we close our ears to the promptings of the Holy Spirit and resist the impulses of grace, then we regress, become spiritually lukewarm and stagnate at a low level of prayer. We become inwardly confused and religiously unsettled.

The prayerful person is responsive to the slightest initiative of the Holy Spirit. The person who is eager to learn the lessons of prayer requires little prompting to submit at once to the action of the Holy Spirit. Such religious are extremely attentive to obedience, to poverty, and to mortification. They never say "no" to their master, the Holy Spirit, who speaks tenderly to them in a language devoid of words, but full of love.

May we never disappoint the Holy Spirit! There is an expression in Latin which is very difficult to translate. It states: *"Et erunt docibles Dei,"* and applies to those who do not disappoint the Holy Spirit. Translated, that would mean: "They will be able to be taught by God." Do we fit that description? I am deeply moved, when I consider that I am not the one who now speaks to you. It is our teacher, the Holy Spirit, who speaks to each one of us in the secret recesses of our hearts. Who knows whether some among us have passed close to the Spirit without hearing his voice or opening our souls to his sweet breath? Therefore, it is urgent for us this very evening to reawaken our religious sensitivity and respect for the Holy Spirit. The Spirit comes to us with his priceless teaching on prayer. Will we fail to welcome him? Would a person sincerely seek to grow in prayer and yet be unwilling to fulfill the necessary conditions and follow the proper instructions?

Would someone set out to be a musical virtuoso, but refuse to do the required practice? A person who learns neither the elements nor the techniques of art, will never progress professionally.

Prayer is actually an art. I will leave you now in the silent presence of the Holy Spirit. If you have ever disappointed the Spirit, from this moment on, be open and welcoming to him. May each one of us tonight say silently, but wholeheartedly, "Come, Holy Spirit." Let us ask the Spirit to fill our souls and to transform our hearts. May we experience a new religious profession and be created anew as students following the instructions of the Holy Spirit, our master of prayer. Amen.

Conference 13
The Apostolate
Saturday Evening

Saint Anselm was a great theologian and saint of the twelfth century. He lived in the famous abbey of Notre Dame du Becq, located between Evreux and Lisieux in Normandy. Saint Anselm wrote a brief theological treatise, entitled: *"Cur Deus Homo"* or, in English, "Why God Became Man."[1] In truth, the Incarnation is a great mystery. A few days ago, I presented a widely held opinion with far-reaching implications. In that light, consider how Adam and Eve, the first man and the first woman, committed a sin, which shattered God's creative masterpiece. As a result of this first sin, they transmitted a certain inner disorder to their descendants, who repeated their sin again and again in a heart-breaking way.

A plant gives glory to God simply by following its nature, even without awareness. The flowers and the birds, the animals and all other creatures give glory to God by simply following their nature. However, the only creature endowed by God with reason, freedom, and greater gifts than any other creature on earth is the very one who rises up in disobedience against God.

Similarly, in the realm of the angels, the one who was most gifted, most intelligent and most favored by God, was the very one who rose up in disobedience and brought along countless others, weaker than himself. In light of the fact that human nature consistently and undeniably tends to debase God's creation, the coming of the Word made flesh took on a completely different character.

The Word made flesh came to restore the original work of God by refashioning what Adam and Eve had disfigured. He reestablished the supernatural plan which had been shattered by the rash action of Adam and Eve. You recall the passage in Paul's "Letter to the Romans," wherein he develops the parallel between the role of the first Adam and the second Adam (Jesus).[2] You recall, too, the passage from Saint Bernard, which parallels the work of the first and second Eve (Mary).[3] The first figures (Adam and Eve) destroyed God's work by their disobedience. The second figures (Jesus and Mary) restored that work by their obedience, demonstrated so painfully, yet poignantly, in the Passion. Christ accordingly came to save the world and to teach us the sure road to true happiness.

Adam and Eve were initially happy. Their human nature was harmoniously balanced. They experienced neither sickness nor death. They relished their physical activities. They worked, but felt no weariness. Rather, their work was a rewarding exercise of their physical prowess and strengthened every tissue of their bodies. In the depths of their hearts they were happy and loved each other without any complications. There was no hint of lust to upset their tender relationship, which in its purity and propriety completely conformed to God's law. On the supernatural level, they were likewise happy, since they were blessed with sanctifying grace. In the poetic imagery of Scripture, "...they heard the Lord God moving about in the garden at the breezy time of the day" [Gen. 3: 8].

Christ came to earth to teach anew the true meaning of happiness, for which the human heart still yearned. We encounter this recurring theme as we listen to Christ's words and follow him each step of the way in the Gospels. Verse after verse, we find this theme: "I came so that they might have life and have it more abundantly" [Jn 10: 10]. In the Gospel of John, Christ explains at length to the crowds whom he had fed the previous day, that they should seek not perishable bread, but the bread that is his body. He even used these words: "...my flesh is true food and my blood is true drink...whoever eats my flesh and drinks my blood has eternal life" [Jn 6: 56 and 54]. He consistently conveys the same theme: "I have come so that they may have peace in the depths of their being."[4] In another text, the Psalmist put this pledge of commitment to the Father on the lips of the Word about to be made flesh: "Sacrifice or oblation you wished not, but ears open to obedience you gave me. Holocausts or sin offerings you sought not; then said I 'Behold I come...to do your will, O my God'..." [Ps 46: 7-9]. The very name of Jesus sums up his entire life's work, since the name Jesus means Savior.

At the outset of the public life of Jesus, Saint John the Baptist enthusiastically points him out to the crowds on the banks of the Jordan in these words: *"Ecce Agnus Dei, ecce qui tollit peccata mundi"* [Jn 1: 29]. Look at this man, unlike all others. He is God's sacrifice, who takes away the sin of the world. In turn, Christ continuously offers himself to us as both victim and savior. As we examine his life, we do not find a self-centered, self-protective person, who is always complaining of being tired and is reluctant to save the world. Rather, we see that his sole concern is redemption, regardless of its demands on him. He came to win salvation and that is what he had to do. When he unavoidably upset his parents and broke out of the close intimacy of his family, he said to his mother: "Did you not know that I must be in my father's house?" [Lk 2: 48].

Later in his life, someone came and told him: "Your mother is outside and would like to speak with you." With the crowd pressing in on him, he points out that he no longer belongs to his mother as a son entrusted to her care and the source of her solace. His heart still stores all the gratitude and tenderness of a devoted son. However, his mother no longer controls his life. Rather, she must now accompany him on his appointed mission. "Those who now constitute my family are the ones who do the will of my Father, for the hour has come for me to complete my mission."[5] His entire life is devoted to this single purpose: "To save others and to tell them what I see in my human nature."[6]

Jesus, our brother, contemplates what no one else has contemplated. Jesus, our brother, thus found true happiness and discovered his mission as well as the real meaning of life. He is deeply troubled to see such a vast number of his brothers and sisters, searching in vain for what he has found. In anguish he ponders how to teach them the truth and show them what nourishes every aspect of his life. How can he convince them of this truth? You are well aware of the moving words he spoke upon seeing the huge crowd that had come in quest of him. He said to the Apostles: "Look at this needy crowd. They are like sheep without a shepherd."[7]

One evening, Jesus was on the northern side of Lake Genesareth on the grassy plain, where he had been preaching all day. As he gazed out on the crowds, someone said to him: "Dismiss the crowds so that they can go to the villages and buy food for themselves." Jesus said to them, "There is no need for them to go away; give them some food yourselves" [Mt 14: 1-16]. He was deeply moved at the sight of such consistently needy crowds. In touching words he spoke of the stray sheep: "The good shepherd, even if he is tired at the end of a long day at work, upon noticing that one of his sheep is missing, takes action. At once, he leaves the others and goes off over hill and dale in search of the lost sheep."[8] Still again, Jesus says: "...there will be more joy in heaven over one sinner who repents than over ninety-nine righteous people who have no need of repentance" [Lk 15: 7]. In a further demonstration of his concern for those in need of the truth, Jesus states: "Those who are healthy do not need a physician, but the sick do. I have not come to call the righteous to repentance, but sinners" [Lk 6: 31-32]. We could continue citing scriptural texts, all of which reveal to us the human heart of Christ, filled with love of God and with an older brother's concern for the rest of his family.

There is only one type of person Jesus criticizes. That type includes the hypocrites, the proud, and the self-righteous. Such persons think that they have found the truth, when, in fact, they have found nothing but themselves. They then feel justified in spitting out condemnation on their sisters and brothers. Such was the Pharisee who prayed aloud: "Lord, I thank you for making me different from others. I am virtuous and holy." At the same time, there was a poor man in the back of the synagogue, who prayed quietly: "Lord, forgive me, for I have done wrong. I am a publican, a tax-collector for the Romans, who are regarded as invaders by the Sanhedrin. Still, I must save my soul. So, if I have done anything unjust, I want to make reparation." This second person goes away forgiven; the first person is like a rot-filled sepulcher and goes away with only his self-centered smugness.[9]

We want to highlight the gracious ease with which Christ pardons those women he meets who have been accused of sins of impurity. Mary Magdalene, the woman taken in adultery, and the Samaritan woman at the well are excellent examples. Christ uses no harsh words of reproach with them. Consider the poor Samaritan woman. God well knows that she has scandalized the whole region. She is a prostitute. Nevertheless, when she meets Christ, he speaks gently to her.[10] He understands that these poor sinners are searching for love, but do not know its true nature. Therefore, they are to be pitied, not condemned.

If we examine Christ's life and listen to his heart, we appreciate that he came to teach others the true meaning of happiness. That is his burning ambition. He is aflame with zeal for the apostolate. He is an apostle from head to toe, for that is his mission.

I would like now to ask you, dear Sisters, the same question Saint Anselm asked: "Why did you come here?" Christ left his father's bosom and came into the world in order to save souls. "Why did you come here?" What did you come to do here in the Carmelite community? Did you come here out of laziness, because it was too trying to do good in the world? Did you come here out of concern for your own salvation, because you were encountering too much temptation in the world? How sad that would be! But, let us suppose that your only reason for coming here was to work out your own salvation. That might have been an adequate reason for the initial stage of a vocation. However, your prayer would be deficient and your life would be pathetic, if you remained on that level.

To the degree that we are united to Christ and God lives in us, Jesus speaks to us about others. Christ is consumed with the apostolate. How can we call ourselves his friends, if we want him to speak to us about anything except the deep distress of countless souls? We have come to know Christ, not by reason of anything we have done, but rather by God's great goodness. Why, we might ask, has God so chosen us and not others? Therein lies the mystery of God's preferential will. Let me try to explain why God has chosen us. The reason is that Christ saw in us potentially generous souls. Perhaps he thought that, if he chose us, we would manifest steadfast spiritual generosity and not calculate its cost in terms of our time, our personal lives, and our egos. How often Christ has been disappointed by priests who have lost their fervor and become dejected? By relying solely on themselves, they grow so discouraged that they cease to be priests, in any real sense. How wretched is the spiritual life of such priests, who offer Mass mechanically and eventually lose all hope!

Consider the disappointment of Christ concerning certain Carmelite sisters who are no longer generous in spirit. Instead, they live worldly lives and have gradually settled into comfortable little niches. They have failed to understand Christ's confidence in them. They devote their attention, not to Christ, but only to themselves. As a result, they are unworthy of Christ's call. By way of contrast, consider the words of our Carmelite saints, for that is what we have come here to do. We have come to Carmel to save the whole world not just some souls. There are other religious communities in which we could devote ourselves to the care of the sick, the elderly, and the orphans. However, we have come to Carmel in order to take the world in our arms and lift it up with all our strength so that it can glimpse God in all his goodness.

Recall our founding father, Elijah! Did he spiritually stir up Palestine or did he sluggishly seek only his own peace and quiet? When God spoke to him at prayer, telling him of the distress of the people of Israel and the sins of their royal rulers, he listened attentively and went off immediately, despite the personal consequences. He trudged across the country, proclaiming truth to those who needed to hear it. He sometimes sparked bitter opposition. He risked his life, but did not waver. He offered his time, his life, his very self, without calculating the cost.

The same was true of Saint John of the Cross and Father Anthony.[11] Recall the little cradle of our Reform. That humble little house exhibited extraordinary poverty. The friars enjoyed no comforts. Their chapel was a loft whose roof tiles let snow in on them during the winter. Nonetheless, they spent long periods there in prayer. Then, each morning they went out to the neighboring villages to proclaim God's goodness. Thus, at the very beginning of our Reform, we discover two hearts aflame with a desire to tell others the secret of Christ's love. In this way, they renewed our apostolic traditions in accordance with their ancient origins.

Now, let us turn our attention to our spiritual mother, Saint Teresa of Avila. You are familiar with her passionate writings concerning Protestants, Calvinism, and heresy in France. Recall how urgently she wanted to come to the aid of those souls who were being lost. Likewise, consider Saint Thérèse of Lisieux. She was seized by a powerful urge to go off on the foreign missions. The missionary magazines which she read made her heart beat with intense emotion. She came to realize, however, that as a Carmelite, her apostolic engagement would be both deeper and wider, since it would be reduced to essentials. At the outset of her religious life, she straightforwardly said: "I have come here to save souls."[12]

How, then, shall we accomplish the work of salvation that awaits us? In regard to these matters, I may seem somewhat demanding. Yet, as you well know, I am not the one who is speaking to you. I am simply conveying to you the words and themes that Christ wants you to hear. Some of you need to listen carefully to this echo of God and all its demands. Take these words to heart, as if they were destined directly to you by God's own mercy.

We must carry out our duty of saving the world and do it first of all by loving and adopting sinners. I deliberately say "love them" and "adopt them." In all honesty, nothing is more distressful to me than to hear about people who do not practice their religion. However, I also hear about professedly charitable men, women, and even religious, who speak shamefully of those who identify themselves as Socialists or Communists. Yet we are ultimately to blame that these people have left the church. It is not their fault; it is ours. We are the culprits; as priests and nuns, we have failed in our mission. We have been unable to make Christ known to them. All who had this responsibility have failed, especially the so-called "elite" with their money, prestige, and social position. We are all responsible for those who have abandoned their religion. We can learn from the example of Don Bosco.[13] His apostolate was singularly successful because he understood and loved the poor. He never viewed them as his enemies, even when they threw stones at him.

Love the Communists. Adopt them. God has providentially permitted me (as a son of working class parents) to become well acquainted with working-class youth. During my military service, during the war, and during my captivity, I was in the midst of workers. As a result, I am well acquainted with Communist and Socialist thinking. I have come to know many mid-level directors of these movements. I have found many first-rate men among them. They are ready to die for their ideal, and have often done so. They regularly devote their time to propagating their ideas and distributing their literature. By way of contrast, I have rarely found the same level of dedication among the "respectable people" who spend their time on boats or at parties and always look for enjoyment, even at work. They never sacrifice themselves for others.

God deeply loves these poor people, who are sincere in their conviction and confident that they serve a good cause. In all honesty, I am convinced that they will be saved! Do not speak disparagingly of them! Do parents speak badly of their children, even if they are wayward? If you love them and adopt them because they are the unfortunate children of the family, you will do them great good. Why not make yourselves their spiritual mothers?

Now, let us examine our consciences. Any Carmelite who is spiritually lukewarm, is apostolically remiss. Are we really fulfilling our duty? In all honesty, are we genuinely faithful and passionately committed to fulfilling all the requirements of our Rule and our Constitutions, because we realize the repercussions of our actions on the world? Every time we turn away from our ideal, we do spiritual harm to others. Are we humble and obedient? Do we practice poverty and mortification? Our Rule is admirably balanced and thus permits a practice of mortification consistent with sound health. Do we mortify ourselves by getting up at the first bell and by conforming to the daily schedule? Do we mortify ourselves in regard to food, clothing, books and the like? Every time we neglect mortification, we do spiritual harm to others. Are we filled with a burning sense of prayer, expressive of an intimate union with Christ? Every time we omit prayer and turn aside from Christ through laziness, we do spiritual harm to others. We could continue this long list indefinitely!

Let us remember this one thing. Throughout his life, Christ was unsparing of himself in his zeal to save souls. Our saints have likewise been zealous to save souls. Consider Saint Thérèse, as she offered her walk in the garden for a missionary. All our saints have been passionate apostles. So, too, must we be. This morning, we are going to make an examination of conscience in this regard. Are we other Christs and other Apostles? Are we true Carmelites? Or, are we not merely living smugly? Are we completely committed to the apostolate and eager to give our all to the souls who await our help?

Do we live in such a way that Christ is not deeply disappointed in us? We want to take care not to shy away from suffering, not to speak impulsively, and not to seek a life of comfort. We want to take care to follow our Rule in its demanding details and not just in its broad outline. In a word, we want to avoid pretending to be Carmelites, and instead to be genuine Carmelites. A pseudo-Carmelite is a pseudo-apostle. In ten, fifteen or thirty more years, you will come before God to render an account of your life. Then, Christ will show you all the souls you should have saved. You will have no valid excuse and will have to reply: "I could not spare my sleep or I was tired..."

True Carmelites are committed to saving the world. Day by day they grow in prayerfulness and year by year they become living embodiments of our Rule and Constitutions. Admittedly, we may be far from perfect at the beginning of our religious life. However, once we have completed our apprenticeship, we must be the living embodiment of our Rule and Constitutions for no other reason than to work with Christ for the salvation of the world. Pray to our saints and to the Virgin Mary to help you to attain that goal. Amen.

Conference 14
Review of the Retreat: To Give Back a Hundredfold
Sunday Evening

We are coming to the end of this retreat. This evening we conclude these days of silence, during which you have been listening very keenly to God's voice. Tomorrow, the routines of daily lives will resume. For one last time, let us join together in a spirit of recollection. For one last time, let us converse together in God's presence. Recall how last night we reflected together on our master of prayer, the Holy Spirit. Tonight, my plan is not to develop a particular theme. Instead, I would prefer simply to draw together the topics we have treated and to encourage each of you to listen to Christ, our teacher, as he speaks personally to you.

Do you recall what we have together seen and considered in this retreat? The main emphasis must be our life of prayer; that must be everything. I have had no time to speak about the Divine Office with you. The heart must be in contact with God during the recitation of the Office. That heart must be filled with prayer and love. Our participation at Mass, our grace-filled actions, our Communions must be religious acts stamped with prayer and love. Our material work of the day must be a work bathed in prayer. Our life is the life of heaven. Saint John of the Cross has said that the contemplative has no task here below that she will not have in heaven.[1] The difference is that on earth that task is done in the obscurity of faith; in heaven there will be no veil between God and us. This is our vocation now. Thus, Carmel is the beginning of heaven.

For this life of prayer to have all its intensity and fullness, it must be wrapped in silence. The soul that does not love silence is a soul not intended for Carmel. A sluggish soul is not worthy of Carmel, for it will never arrive at profound prayer. Silence, a loyal silence in God's presence all day long, a silence in the depth of one's heart, on one's lips, about oneself, everywhere! Carmel should be called the Monastery of Grand Silence, like the Cistercian monasteries. This is God's silence, because it allows us to listen to the One who reveals God to us, the Holy Spirit. The breath of the Holy Spirit is too delicate to be exposed to noise or exterior agitation. If we know how to welcome silence, it will disclose, little by little, the great mystery of Christ through which we can embrace God! There is so much I still have to say to you about Christ, especially about his Incarnation for us in the Eucharist. The Word Incarnate is always there for us in the Eucharist. This overpowering mystery allows the unworthy hands of the priest to hold the same Body of Christ that the Virgin Mary held in her arms and pressed to her heart. Yet it is the same Christ! The priest takes Christ in his hands and gives him to others! When you receive him, you are like the Virgin Mary during the months she carried her child. You truly carry Christ within you and want to be absorbed in profound thanksgiving. You carry him living within you! How necessary is silence so that the Holy Spirit can reveal to us the grandeur of this mystery.

Christ lives also in the authority that commands in his name. Recall all his lessons and the lessons of the apostolate that we have shared. You must not listen superficially; instead, engrave those lessons on your soul. Dear Sisters, these moments we have spent together truly involved souls touching one another. My soul heard the replies of your souls. In the measure I was speaking, I was overcome to discover the good will in each of your souls. While speaking to you, my soul touched yours. You are souls of good will, but good will is not everything. Our Holy Mother says, "hell is paved with good intentions." You know, from personal experience perhaps, that one can begin generously, but then monotony can nibble away and, little by little, reduce to dust even the greatest fervor. It is nothing to make a good retreat. It is everything to complete a good year and a good life and eventually arrive at death without ever drawing back or losing anything of that first fervor.

I am going to review with you some of the parables, which Jesus spoke to the crowds, who were, like you, filled with enthusiasm and good will. Those crowds followed after our Lord. On Palm Sunday, they hailed him, spreading their garments and their palm branches beneath his feet. A week later, they were insulting him and spitting in his face.

With a sense of sorrow in his words, Christ also spoke to the Apostles, as they made their way together across the fields of Galilee. Looking out on the farmers, as they carefully cultivated their typically small plots, Jesus said: "The Kingdom of Heaven is like a sower, who went out to sow his seed. Some seed fell on a rocky road. Some fell on weedy soil. Some fell on fair, but shallow soil. Finally, some fell on good, rich soil. The birds of the sky came and took the seed that fell on the road; it did not sprout. In the spring, the seed that fell in the weedy soil, did sprout, but the weeds were stronger than the seed and choked it. In the shallow soil, resting on a layer of rocks, the seed sprouted up like grass. However, with the first hot spell in May, those shoots withered and turned into straw. Finally, the good soil made it possible for the grain of wheat to grow, to strengthen and to produce a hundredfold crop."[2]

Christ went on to explain this parable. God sows his word in every soul. The seed as well as the act of sowing remain objectively the same on God's part. What differs is the fact that all souls are not equally receptive. Shallow, fickle, meddlesome souls are like a road open to every passerby and are always eager for the latest news. The seed remains in them only a few days at best and then is quickly swept away by all who cross their path. The seed that falls on weedy soil symbolizes the soul of genuine good will, who welcomes the seed with joy, but on the following day lets it be choked off by invasive weeds. Such a soul is unwilling to do what has to be done, that is, to tackle the problem at its roots by overcoming tendencies toward troublemaking and rash judgment, egotism and worldliness, moaning and groaning. God's word springs up in such a soul, but other influences are stronger and soon squelch God's word. There is the semblance of spiritual conversion, but that process is too difficult for such a soul.

The seed that falls on the shallow soil, just above a layer of rock, symbolizes the well-intentioned soul that still resists self-surrender. In the religious life, such souls have not been permeated by their vows nor have they worked wholeheartedly at their fulfillment. There is something deep down in their hearts that they refuse to surrender. The seed grows promisingly in such a situation. The prospects seem favorable. However, that obstacle deep down in the heart soon stifles God's word, which could have been very fruitful.

Finally, there are those souls who abandon themselves completely to God's action. They are like fertile soil in the farmer's hands, ready to be plowed. What superb soil! What fine harvests it will produce! But take note of this point: in Christ's explanation, very little seed falls on good soil and almost all the rest is lost.

Perhaps some of us would be upset at the thought of examining the years, be they ten, twenty or fifty that we have spent in religious life. Such persons would likely say: "It seems to me that, upon hearing the message God has sent me during this retreat, I must acknowledge my failure to be faithful up to this point in time." It is to just such persons that Christ addresses the parable of "The Workers in the Vineyard" [Mt 20: 1-16]. In that parable, some workers were hired late in the day, when there was little time left to work. At the end of the day, the master instructed the foreman that all the workers should receive the same pay. The master wanted to show by this gesture that we can rectify a situation by the strength of our love and fidelity. So it is, that God himself rectifies any deficiencies the soul previously and carelessly caused.[3]

I want once again to share with you a few memorable words, drawn from Blaise Pascal, who generously gave himself over to Christ, the focal point of his profound meditation. In his work, "The Mystery of Jesus," Pascal portrays Christ speaking in his agony and saying to each of us: "I thought of you in my agony. I shed those drops of blood for you." How true! In addition, Pascal writes: "Jesus will be in agony until the end of the world; we must not sleep during that time."[4] In this sense, Christ says to us, as he said with a heavy heart to his Apostles: "So you could not keep watch with me for one hour?"

In the Gospel of our Mass this morning, there was a scathing reproach for all of us. Did you take note of the words of Jesus, when he met the ten lepers? He said: "Go, show yourselves to the priests" [Lk 17: 14]. The law required that the priests confirm their cure. While they were on the way to see the priest, they realized that they had actually been healed. Of the ten lepers, only one came back. He threw himself at the Lord's feet and thanked him. Christ then asked him: "Ten were cleansed, were they not? Where are the other nine?" [Lk 17: 17]. Luke then points out that the one leper who did return was, in fact, a Samaritan. In today's language, we would say the nine were smugly self-righteous, while the other one was a social outcast.

What are we really like? To which group do we belong? To those who forget or to those who express gratitude?

Finally, please, take as a spiritual souvenir of this entire retreat and recall each day how I have spoken to you as a brother. Whenever I address you as "my dear Sisters," these words are not a mere formality, but are rather a genuine expression of my sincere affection for you. We actually are members of the same family. I have been ordained to the priesthood. It is in this capacity that I have made myself available to you. I have spoken with you as my responsibility requires. It is now up to you to fulfill your responsibility. That is a matter between you and God. My task has been completed; your task is just beginning! I have called you, "my dear Sisters," because, in addition, I owe you such a debt of gratitude for all your kindness to the College.[5] I have sought to express my appreciation by helping you to come to a richer understanding of our shared Carmelite ideal. There is no greater gift I can offer you than a deeper awareness of God's love. I hope that, every morning and every evening, as you recite the Office, from today until your next retreat, you will pay special attention to its concluding words. Whenever you come upon these words, check to see if you are keeping your retreat resolutions.

Every day we chant these words: *"Hodie si vocem ejus audieritis nolite obdurare corda vestra!;* Oh, that today you would hear his voice: Harden not your hearts..."[6] Each day, when you make your examination of conscience, ask yourself: "Am I holding fast to my retreat resolutions or am I letting them lapse?"

"*Hodie, si vocem eius audieritis, nolite obdurare corda vestra!*"

May these words form a bond between your soul and mine throughout the year ahead. I promise to remember each one of you in prayer during the daily recitation of Matins. I urge you to bear in mind that the words you have heard in this retreat are God's words. If you found anything in your spiritual life that needs to be clarified, corrected or cut out, hold fast to your resolution and inspiration, as expressions of God's enduring love.

"Oh, that today you would hear his voice: Harden not your hearts..." Amen.

Notes

CONFERENCE 1

1. For a complete biography of Père Jacques in English, see Francis J. Murphy, *Père Jacques: Resplendent in Victory* (Washington, D.C.: ICS Publications, 1998). The indispensable source in French is Philippe de la Trinité, *Le Père Jacques: Martyr de la Charité.* (Paris: Desclée de Brouwer, 1947). "Etudes Carmélitaines" series.
2. Throughout this retreat, Père Jacques tends to use the expression: "le Bon Dieu" in speaking of God. While this expression, meaning literally "the Good God," reflects pious French usage of the period, it seems more suitable in English to say simply "God."
3. See H. Tristram, ed., *John Henry Newman Autobiographical Writings* (New York: Sheed and Ward, 1957), 125.
4. On the relationship of the prophet Elijah to the origins and charism of the Carmelite order, see P.T. Rohrbach, *Journey to Carith: The Story of the Carmelite Order* (Garden City, N.Y.: Doubleday & Company, 1966), 18-39.
5. Saint John of the Cross (1542-1591) was one of the pioneers of the male Carmelite reform in Spain and remains esteemed as one of the greatest spiritual theologians in the history of the Church.
6. "La Chartreuse" is the first monastery of the Carthusian order, founded in 1084 in southern France.
7. Saint Teresa of Avila (1515-1582) led the Carmelite reform in Spain, worked closely with Saint John of the Cross and was a prolific spiritual writer.
8. Saint Thérèse of Lisieux (1873-1897), popularly called the "Little Flower," was a Carmelite nun, who became remarkably revered following her death at a young age, due to the extraordinary appeal of her posthumously published autobiography, *Story of a Soul.*

9. Sister Marie-Angélique (1893-1919) was a celebrated concert pianist, who renounced her professional career in 1914, becoming a Carmelite at Pontoise in the very convent where this retreat took place.
10. Reference is made here to Thomas à Kempis (1380-1471), author of the spiritual classic, *The Imitation of Christ.*
11. See *Sketch of the Mount* in John of the Cross, *The Collected Works of St. John of the Cross,* rev. ed. trans. Kieran Kavanaugh, O.C.D. and Otilio Rodriguez, O.C.D. (Washington, DC: ICS Publications, 1991), 110-111.
12. Saint Bernard (1090-1153) was a renowned medieval French theologian and founding abbot of the Cistercian monastery of Clairvaux.

CONFERENCE 2

1. This self-effacing comment refers to Père Jacques's role as headmaster of the Petit-Collège d'Avon and is an indication of his dry sense of humor.
2. John of the Cross, *Sayings of Light and Love*, 60 in *Collected Works*, 90.
3. The title Curé of Ars is the popular designation of Saint John Vianney (1786-1859), an outstanding, yet simple parish priest, noted for his pastoral dedication and personal piety.
4. This adage is familiar in English as: "Out of sight, out of mind." The original source of this saying is: Thomas à Kempis, *The Imitation of Christ*, Book 1, Chapter 23.
5. This episode from the life of Saint Francis of Assisi (1182-1226) is recounted in Julien Green, *God's Fool: The Life and Times of Francis of Assisi*, trans. Peter Heinegg (San Francisco: Harper & Row, 1985), 70-71.
6. The bracketed material in this passage is most likely an addition inserted by the stenographer.
7. This quotation is a conflation of two scriptural texts: 1 Pet. 3:21 and 1 Tim. 4:12.
8. Here three texts from the Gospel of John are woven together: Jn 3:35, 1:14, and 1:16.
9. Here again is a conflation of scriptural texts: Jn 17:24 and 1 Jn 1:13.
10. The book here indicated is: Marie-Vincent Bernadot, *From Holy Communion to the Blessed Trinity*, trans. Francis Izard (Westminster, MD: Newman Press, 1926).

CONFERENCE 3

1. The text cited is from the Common of the Dedication of a Church. The Gospel is taken from Lk 19:1-10, to which are added elements from Lk 18:22. September 7 was the anniversary of the dedication of the Chapel at the Carmel of Pontoise.
2. John of the Cross, *Ascent of Mount Carmel*, 1, 11, 4, in *Collected Works*, 143.
3. These are the concluding words of the Canon in the Mass of the Roman Rite in Latin.
4. Saint Margaret Mary Alacoque (1647-1690) was a Visitation nun, whose visions were catalysts for the development of devotion to the Sacred Heart of Jesus.
5. This form of devotion, often termed "prayer of simple regard," is treated at length in Conference 12.
6. See John of the Cross, *The Dark Night* in *Collected Works*, 358-457.
7. Mk 15:34; translated in English as, "My God, my God, why have you forsaken me?"

CONFERENCE 4

1. Although this conference was given on Tuesday evening, the feast of the Nativity of the Blessed Virgin Mary, celebrated on Wednesday (September 8), had already begun with first Vespers, chanted on Tuesday afternoon.
2. For example, see Lk 5: 15, 16.
3. The convent of the Discalced Carmelite nuns at Beas (Spain) was especially important in the life of Saint John of the Cross. See *God Speaks in the Night: The Life, Times and Teaching of St. John of the Cross* (Washington, D.C.: ICS Publications, 1991), 191-198.
4. On the nature and centrality of the Rule in Carmelite life, see *The Carmelite Directory of the Spiritual Life* (Chicago: The Carmelite Press, 1951), 118-119.
5. Père Jacques is here adapting John of the Cross, "The Living Flame of Love" 3.28 in *Collected Works*, 620.
6. Reference here is made to an episode recounted *in Story of a Soul: The Autobiography of St. Thérèse of Lisieux*, trans. John Clarke, O.C.D. (Washington, D.C.: ICS Publications, 1976), 27.

7. This episode is recounted in: S. Navantes, *The Imitation of St. Thérèse of the Child Jesus,* trans. Sister Mary Grace, O.Carm. (Chicago: Franciscan Herald Press, 1979), 81-82.
8. In this regard, see Federico Ruiz, "Farewell to His Brother" in *God Speaks in the Night*, 338-341. There is inserted at this point in the transcription of the text of the retreat, a sentence enclosed in parentheses and added most likely by the stenographer. It reads: "Lord, let me die alone in a monastery where I am neither known nor loved."

CONFERENCE 5

1. Reference here is made to both the anniversary of the dedication of the Chapel of the Carmelite Convent at Pontoise on September 7 and the feast of the Birth of the Virgin Mary on September 8.
2. This Breviary text is from the Magnificat Antiphon for Second Vespers from the Common of the Dedication of a Church.
3. For a fuller explanation of this usage, see Dom Columba Marmion, *Sponsa Verbi: The Virgin Consecrated to Christ,* trans. Francis Izard (St. Louis: B. Herder, 1925).
4. The text cited in this passage is actually from Proverbs, which in liturgical usage at that time was designated as a subdivision of the Book of Wisdom.
5. In this paragraph Père Jacques uses and paraphrases excerpts from Prov. 8:22-35.
6. This text is referred to as an Epistle, which term was traditionally applied to the first scripture reading of the Mass prior to the liturgical reforms of Vatican Council II.
7. Jacques-Marie Monsabré, O.P. (1827-1907) was a Dominican theologian and a noted preacher.
8. This text is, in fact, from Dan. 3:52-57 and is used in the Office of Sunday at Lauds.
9. Nestorius was Patriarch of Constantinople (428-431) and taught that God the Son and Jesus the man were two distinct persons. The Council of Ephesus condemned his teaching as heretical in 431 and Nestorius was then deposed.
10. Responsory, Sixth Lesson, Matins for the Nativity of the Lord.
11. Saint Alphonsus Ligouri (1696-1787) was an Italian priest, renowned as an outstanding preacher and moral theologian. He founded the Congregation of the Most Holy Redeemer, popularly called the Redemptorists.

12. Lk 1:38, translated in English as: "May it be done to me according to your word."

CONFERENCE 6

1. September 8 was also celebrated locally as the feast of Notre Dame de Pontoise, known also as Notre Dame de Santé.
2. Saint Catherine of Siena (1347-1380) was a Dominican nun, noted for her spiritual writings and her efforts to reform the Church.
3. In English: "Behold, I am the handmaid of the Lord" [Lk 1:38].

CONFERENCE 7

1. This quotation can be found in context in: Rt. Rev. E. Bougaud, *Life of Saint Margaret Mary Alacoque* (New York: Benziger Brothers, 1920), 175-179.
2. See Conference 1, footnote 11.
3. In English: "Why have you come here?"
4. Here Père Jacques is paraphrasing Jn 12:24.
5. See 2 Cor. 4:7.
6. Saint Ignatius Loyola (1491-1556) was the founder of the Society of Jesus, more familiarly called the Jesuits, and the author of *The Spiritual Exercises*.
7. The Book of Job in the Hebrew Bible recounts the sufferings of Job in their fullness.
8. Here Père Jacques is paraphrasing Mt 25: 1-13.
9. See E.G. Gardner, ed. and trans., *The Book of Saint Bernard on the Love of God* (New York: E.P. Dutton, 1915), 68-69.
10. A second, alternative conclusion to this conference is added at this point. However, that addition is most likely a pious reflection by the stenographer and not by Père Jacques.

CONFERENCE 8

1. Reference here is made to the Shroud of Turin, which has been widely believed since the 16th century to be the actual burial cloth of Jesus.
2. The full episode of the Transfiguration, alluded to here, is recounted in Mt 1:1-8.
3. Blaise Pascal (1623-1662) was a brilliant mathematician, philosopher and writer. This quotation is from his *Pensées*, trans. A.J. Krailsheimer (Baltimore: Penguin Books, 1966), 95, no. 201.

4. See William of St. Thierry et al., *St. Bernard of Clairvaux*, trans. G. Webb and A. Walker (Westminster, MD: Newman Press, 1960), 42.
5. For a fuller account of this period, see *God Speaks in the Night*, 157-177.
6. Cf. Mt 25:1-13.
7. Charles de Foucauld (1858-1916) was a French military officer, who renounced his life of luxury to become a Trappist priest and eventually a hermit among the Arab Moslems of North Africa. His example inspired the foundation of three religious communities.
8. This is the most explicit reference made in this retreat to World War II, then at its height.

CONFERENCE 9

1. This quotation conflates elements from: Lk 4:43; Mt 11:5 and Jn 10:38.
2. Here Père Jacques adapts words drawn from Mt 23:3.
3. This exchange takes place, in fact, before Pilate, not Caiaphas.
4. This quotation is an adaptation of Rom. 13:1-7.

CONFERENCE 10

1. Père Jacques is alluding here to the infamous roundup of the Jews of Paris on July 16, 1942.
2. The feast of the Seven Sorrows of the Blessed Virgin Mary is celebrated annually on September 15.
3. Père Jacques here refers to the painting, "Saint Francis Embracing Christ on the Cross" by the Spanish artist Bartolomé Murillo (1617-1682). The painting now hangs in the Museo Provincial, Toledo.
4. In English: "either to die or to suffer."
5. This quotation is adapted from: *The Book of Her Life* in *The Collected Works of St. Teresa of Avila*, vol. 1, trans. by Kieran Kavanaugh, O.C.D. and Otilio Rodriguez, O.C.D. (Washington, D.C.: ICS Publications, 1976), 283.

CONFERENCE 11

1. This text, based on 1 Cor. 13: 8-13, is now used as Antiphon 6 (formerly Antiphon 7) in the ceremony of the Washing of Feet in the Mass of the Lord's Supper on Holy Thursday.
2. Charles Péguy (1873-1914) was a celebrated French patriot and religious poet, who was killed in World War I. This passage is adapted

from his work "Hope" in *Men and Saints: Prose and Poetry,* trans. by A. and J. Green (New York: Pantheon Books, 1944), 233-249.

3. The expression the "Good God" ("Bon Dieu" in French) is not customarily used in English.
4. See *St. Thérèse of Lisieux: Her Last Conversations,* trans. by John Clarke, O.C.D. (Washington, D.C.: ICS Publications, 1977), 102.
5. The reference here is to Saint Thomas Aquinas (1225-1274), an Italian Dominican priest, generally considered to be the greatest theologian in the history of Christianity.
6. Père Jacques here paraphrases a familiar passage from *Story of a Soul*, 136.
7. See Jean-Pierre de Caussade, *Abandonment to Divine Providence,* trans. by J. Beevers (Garden City, NY: Image Books, 1975).
8. In English these Latin words literally mean a "taste" and "to digest."
9. Here Père Jacques is adapting a text from *The Collected Works of St. Teresa of Avila*, vol. 1, 168.
10. Paraphrase of Jas 1:17.
11. This prayer, composed by Père Jacques, reflects Teresian themes cited earlier.

CONFERENCE 12

1. Maurice Landrieu, *The Forgotten Paraclete,* trans. E. Leahy (New York: Benizger, 1924).
2. Here Père Jacques is adapting a text from *The Collected Works of St. Teresa of Avila*, vol. 1, 96.
3. The Curé of Ars is the popular name of St. John Vianney (1786-1859), a diocesan priest renowned for his personal piety and pastoral dedication.
4. This quotation is a conflation of Jn 16: 7 and Jn 14:26.
5. That dissertation was subsequently published in English as: Froget, Barthélemey, *The Indwelling of the Holy Spirit in the Souls of the Just according to the Teaching of Saint Thomas Aquinas,* trans. S. Raemers (Westminster, MD: Newman Press, 1952).

CONFERENCE 13

1. Saint Anselm of Canterbury, *Why God Became Man and The Virgin Conception and Original Sin*, trans. J. Colleran (Albany, NY: Magi Books, 1969).
2. Rom. 5: 12-21.

3. See "Second Sermon on the Glories of the Mother of God" in *St. Bernard's Sermons on the Blessed Virgin Mary,* trans. A priest of Mount Melleray. (Chulmleigh, UK: Augustine Publishing Co., 1984), 16-18.
4. Here Père Jacques is adapting Jn 10: 10 and Jn 12: 47.
5. This reflection is drawn from Mt 12: 47-50.
6. Père Jacques is not making a direct quotation here, but is rather placing these words on the lips of Jesus.
7. Here Père Jacques is paraphrasing Mt 9: 36.
8. This quotation is an adaptation of Mt 18: 12.
9. Here Père Jacques is adapting Lk 18: 9-14.
10. The story of the Samaritan woman is found in Jn 4: 4-26.
11. Father Anthony of Jesus was one of the original members of the reformed male Carmelites along with Saint John of the Cross. Their difficulties, alluded to here, are described in P.T. Rohrbach, *Journey to Carith*, 161-168.
12. See *Story of a Soul*, Chapter 7, 149.
13. Saint John Bosco (1815-1888), popularly called Don Bosco, was an Italian priest known for his extraordinary dedication to poor youth.

CONFERENCE 14

1. Here Père Jacques perhaps has in mind John of the Cross's commentary on stanza 28 of the *Spiritual Canticle*; see *Collected Works*, 583-586.
2. This quotation is a paraphrase of Mt 13: 1-8.
3. In the transcription of this conference, this same theme is repeated in words enclosed in parentheses and inserted, most likely by the stenographer.
4. Blaise Pascal, *Pensées*, 334.
5. The reference here is to the Petit-Collège d'Avon, a Carmelite boarding school, of which Père Jacques was Headmaster.
6. This verse, drawn from Ps. 94: 8 is the Invitatory for Matins in the Ordinary of the Divine Office.

The Institute of Carmelite Studies promotes research and publication in the field of Carmelite spirituality. Its members are Discalced Carmelites, part of a Roman Catholic community—friars, nuns, and laity—who are heirs to the teaching and way of life of Teresa of Jesus and John of the Cross, men and women dedicated to contemplation and to ministry in the Church and the world. Information concerning their way of life is available through local diocesan Vocation Offices or from the Vocation Directors' Offices:

5345 S. University Avenue, Chicago, IL 60615

2131 Lincoln Road, NE, Washington, DC 20002-1199

PO Box 3420, San Jose, CA 95156-3420

5151 Marylake Drive, Little Rock, AR 72206-9436